⊰ ACCLAIM FOR ⊱

Ending Elder Abuse: A Family Guide

"This beautiful book is a family love story, filled with practical suggestions and information on caring for an aging loved one. A must read for adult children of aging parents."

> —Pamala D. McGovern, Executive Director, Council on Aging,
> Orange County, Santa Ana, California

"An important story that deserves to be told. Diane Sandell's courage is an inspiration, and her efforts to find solutions show what needs to be done."

> —Kent Shocknek, Anchor, *Today in L.A.*, KNBC-TV, Los Angeles

"...an important and timely book that opens our eyes to the horror of elder abuse; offers constructive, positive step-by-step plans of actions for families, the long-term care facilities and the medical profession."

> —Mary Allen, Former President, Board of Directors,
> Orange County Council of Aging,
> Ombudsman Program, Irvine, California

"(Sandell's) individual efforts have made a difference in many lives over a considerable period of time...I can enthusiastically endorse (this book) as a much needed document."

> —Ruth Cambron, Ombudsman Program Consultant,
> California Department of Aging, Sacramento, California

"...valiant, noble and eloquent efforts on behalf of senior citizens...residents of long term care facilities."

> —Marc B. Hankin, Esquire,
> Attorney at Law, Los Angeles, California

"...confront(s) bravely and boldly the terrible secret of the abused frail elderly of our nation...This book should wake many people up and... undoubtedly will save many lives."

> —The Rev. Dr. Stephen H. Janssen, Senior Minister
> Eastminster Presbyterian Church, Marietta, Georgia

—⧊—

"...a positive approach to inform the public of the issues and their rights, and to offer practical help for everyone who seeks to deal with the provider and patient care-giver issues relating to our own aging bodies as well as of those we love."

—John Crandall, Pastor,
Cornerstone Bible Church, Orange, California

"[This] book will be of tremendous value to the millions of families faced with the dilemma of having to place their elderly loved ones in long-term care facilities, and to those whose loved ones have suffered abuse in these facilities."

—Chris J. Van Ruiten, President, Leisure Consultants, Inc.

"THE BOOK to read about caregiving for our elderly loved ones. [It] will no doubt be welcomed by all who provide services to the elderly, but it will have even greater value for those who have yet to realize the challenges that lie ahead.

—Donna J. Vohar, Attorney at Law, Conway, Pennsylvania

Your book on this subject will be an inspiration as well as an educational guide for dealing with this unpleasant subject in a positive manner. Thank you for giving me the opportunity to share in this endeavor by offering my wholehearted endorsement.

—Randa R. Mendenhall, Marketing Director,
Reston Town Center, Reston, Virginia

"Your very personal story, delivered in a loving and powerful manner, will touch many hearts and drive people to take a stand and make the changes that we as a society need to make. You are a beacon of hope."

—Linda Scheck, Executive Director
Alzheimer's Association of Orange County, Orange, California

"This book will change the lives of those who read it."

—Sandra Ann Hagan, Director, NOBLE Network Outreach—
Better Living for the Elderly, Orange, California

ENDING
ELDER ABUSE
⇥ A FAMILY GUIDE ⇤

DIANE S. SANDELL & LOIS HUDSON

HOW YOU CAN
protect your loved ones ◆ *evaluate facilities*
partner with the medical community ◆ *take care of yourself*
motivate legislators and government officials

AND WHAT TO DO IF THINGS GO WRONG

QED
Press
FORT BRAGG
CALIFORNIA

PUBLISHED BY
QED Press
155 Cypress Street
Fort Bragg, California 95437
(707) 964-9520
Fax: (707)-964-7531
http://www.cypresshouse.com

Ending Elder Abuse: A Family Guide

Book production by Cypress House
Cover by Gopa Illustration & Design
Cover photograph © Photodisc
Printed in Canada
2 4 6 8 9 7 5 3
First edition

Library of Congress Cataloging-in Publication Data
Sandell, Diane S., 1937
Ending elder abuse: a family guide / Diane S. Sandell and
Lois Hudson. p. cm.
Includes index.
ISBN 0-936609-41-9
1. Aged—Abuse of—United States. 2. Aging parents—
Abuse of—United States. 3. Nursing home patients—Abuse of—United
States. 4. Aging parents—Care—United States.
5. Aging parents—United States—Family relationships. 6. Adult children
of aging parents—United States—Family relationships. 7. Adult children
of aging parents—United States—Attitudes. I. Hudson, Lois., 1933
11. Title.
HV6626.3 S26 2000
362.6—dc21
00-033312

DEDICATED TO

⚬ BESSIE AND VIRGIE ⚬

Two of a Kind

DISCLAIMER

❧ This book was created to provide information on safeguarding elders from abuse. It is sold with the understanding that the publisher and authors are not engaged in rendering legal or other professional services. If legal or other expert assistance is required, the advice of competent professionals should be sought.

It is not the purpose of this book to reprint all the material that is otherwise available to those in need of information on the subject of elder abuse prevention. The information herein is derived from the authors' personal experience, and is intended to complement, supplement, and amplify the existing body of literature pertaining to elder abuse. You are urged to read all the available material, learn as much as possible about the subject, and tailor the information to your individual needs. For more information, please explore the many resources available in your local library and on the Internet.

There is no quick, simple formula for preventing elder abuse. Those who wish to become involved in this complex and sometimes-frustrating subject must expect to invest considerable time and energy in order to derive the maximum benefit, both for caregivers and the elders so needful of their caring.

Every effort has been made to make this book as complete and as accurate as possible. However, there may be mistakes, both typographical and in content. Therefore, this text should be used as a general guide, and not as the only source of information about elder abuse. Furthermore, this book may contain information that is current only up to the printing date.

The purpose of this book is to educate, comfort, and inspire. The authors and QED Press shall have neither liability nor responsibility to any person or entity with respect to any loss or damage caused, or alleged to have been caused, directly or indirectly, by the information contained in this book.

If you do not wish to be bound by the above, you may return this book to the publisher for a full refund.

Contents

Foreword viii

Acknowledgments ix

Introduction xi

Prologue 1

One — One Night's Nightmare 7

Two — Turn Around, Turn Around 19

Three — Get the Hell Out of Dodge 29

Four — Over the River and Through the Woods 37

Five — 5/3 Turkey 43

Six — Tip of the Iceberg 51

Seven — There Ought to Be A Law 57

Eight — A National Disgrace 63

Nine — We Go Public 71

Ten — Meeting Millie and Mrs. Bush 77

Epilogue — Bessie's Legacy 85

Eleven — Attention, Please, Families 87

Twelve — Attention, Please, Physicians
and Medical Personnel 97

Thirteen — Attention, Please,
Administrators and Corporate Management 103

Fourteen — Attention, Please,
Legislators and Government Officials 111

Fifteen — Evaluating Your Elder's Care 119

Sixteen — Coping with the Dirty Dozen 133

Seventeen — You'll Never Walk Alone 157

Appendices 172

Index 198

FOREWORD

As humanity continues to evolve in its understanding of the aging process and the treatment and cure of the various ailments that affect life expectancy, we anticipate an ever-increasing population of senior citizens. The proper care of these men and women presents a challenge to all in our society, not only because they have served us as our caregivers and have earned the right to reciprocation, but also because each of us may find ourselves in the same situation, as elders needing care.

Diane Sandell's and Lois Hudson's book on elder abuse addresses a subject that has been, but must no longer be, overlooked. Their experience in dealing with the subject of the abuse of our senior population has involved personal family members, health care givers, including physicians and institutions involved in elder care, advocacy groups for improved elder care, the media, and our country's lawmakers. They approach a subject uncomfortable to many in a sensitive and factual fashion calling upon personal experience and offering advice both educational and pragmatic that is useful to every level of caregiver and policy maker.

Ivan R. Nichols, M.D.
Orange, California

ACKNOWLEDGMENTS

We, the authors, wish to express our appreciation to our families:
To my husband, Jim, who stands alone, my gift, who was, and is, always there through better or worse, forever, my love; to my sister, Betty Lane, who has walked the years with me, with deep appreciation and respect, my love.

To my children , who always stand by me:
Kathy Lane and Jim, Mark and Dorie, Kimberly and Jon, always, my love; to my grandchildren, Brittney, Rebecca, Patrick, Kevin, and James,

$XXXOOO$, 5/3.
DSS

To my family:
Roger, in remembrance; Jim and Kathy and Patrick; Bob and Heidi, thank you, with love.

LH

To the following, for their encouragement, support, and assistance:
Carole Herman, Foundation Aiding the Elderly, mentor and colleague; Pamala D. McGovern and Rochelle Woolery, Orange County Council on Aging—Ombudsman Ivan R. Nichols, M.D.; Donald R. Gilchrist, Wendy J. Lee, and Ann Abajian, for assistance in legislative areas. Linda Scheck, Orange County Chapter Alzheimer's Association; Ruth Cambron, California Ombudsman Program Consultant; Julie Schoen, California Health Insurance Counseling Advocacy Program; Keith D. Wisbaum, Attorney at Law, specializing in Elder Abuse litigation; Ann Simons, for her beautiful poem; And to the many others, without whom none of this would have been possible, *Thank you.*

To the following at QED Press for their faith and patient assistance in making an impossible dream come true:

Cynthia Frank, Joe Shaw, Mike Brechner and Hannah Cochran

To those who have graciously endorsed our work.

The publisher wishes to thank these individuals and businesses for their generous help with this book:

Michael E. Brown, M.D., John T. Wallace, M.D., and Joe Curren, Executive Director of the Fort Bragg Senior Center, for their invaluable comments on the manuscript; Michele Rubin and Alia Levine, of Writers House, for their encouragement; Sal Glynn, for his publishing expertise and wise counsel; Gopa Design and Illustration, for characteristic grace under pressure, and the staff of QED Press, for their dedication and perseverance.

INTRODUCTION

We wrote this book for families
We wrote this book to give hope and encouragement to families and caregivers of the elderly. It feels like a lonely place, but you don't have to face the maze of elder care alone. While each family must take responsibility for its own aging generation, there are areas of common ground which, when shared, can lighten the load. We've been where you are. The two of us have experienced many years of overseeing and hands-on elder care in our own families, and advocacy for others in similar situations. Those years have provided us with practical, creative problem-solving experience. Let us help you cope with the monotony of the daily care or the sudden trauma of the unexpected crisis.

We wrote this book for the public
Abuse of the elderly does happen, not only in private homes, but also in all kinds of facilities for long-term care. That it happens at all is shocking; that it happens with such frequency is an appalling national disgrace. Every person in the nation and in the world faces the prospect of growing old and perhaps frail. We cannot assume that "it won't happen to me." Awareness and preparation and proactive involvement in one's own future can go far toward safeguarding that future.

We wrote this book for professionals
From years of dialogue with other advocates, medical professionals, long-term care industry managers, legal advocates, and legislators, we offer creative solutions to problems, from the standpoint of both the professionals and the families involved in elder care. There are measures that professionals can initiate and steps that families can encourage. Cooperative effort can ensure a better future for all of us.

BESSIE LANE
1919

DAVID JARVIS
1919

BESSIE LANE
1918

PROLOGUE

᭓ Are you aware that we in the United States of America bear a national disgrace? Would you believe that grandmas are being beaten? Would you be outraged if your grandpa had a leg amputated because of a neglected decubitis ulcer (bedsore)? Or that your aunt had to go to a psychiatric facility for detoxification because she was overmedicated in a long-term care facility? Or that your mom was left alone all night in a wheelchair in the recreation room of another facility?

What would it take to convince you that these things are happening with frightening frequency all across our country? Would it have to happen to someone you love?

I wasn't aware of it. Then it happened to my mom. I was convinced. I wanted it never to happen to anyone else. I had to do something. All I knew to do was to tell her story.

᭓᭓

SHE WAS A SURVIVOR.

Bessie Lane was born February 26, 1897, one of seven children of working-class parents. Though times were often difficult, she was raised in an era when people did what they had to do, with quiet strength and dignity. The one iron rule from her childhood was, "Always be a lady—whatever the circumstances," and Bessie faced life head-on with optimism, warmth, and love. She was a lady.

I

Though she was "never sick a day" in her young life, Bessie had an aura of delicate fragility that made people want to take care of her. When her father's affluent—but—childless brother and his wife offered to help the family by taking one of the children into their home in nearby Bridgeport, Connecticut, it was sixteen-year-old Bessie who was chosen to go.

Bessie not only survived the separation from her family; she thrived in the genteel atmosphere of her aunt and uncle's home. She finished her schooling and entered the business world of Uncle Charlie's ice cream and candy factory, Lane's Confectionery, where she was hostess and cashier. Her lifelong love of sweet treats began during this time, when she was allowed the privilege of tasting all the flavors of candy and ice cream. No matter how many she tried, strawberry ice cream remained her favorite.

Although Bessie's new station in life afforded her many enjoyable benefits, such as being driven to work by Aunt Mame's chauffeur, she never let it go to her head, never lost her sense of humor or her dignity. One day, when a clique of obviously wealthy girls sought to put her down by placing their long, complicated order in French, Bessie smiled deferentially and disappeared through the swinging doors to the kitchen. The snide giggling ceased abruptly when Bessie, who understood French, appeared in an incredibly short time with the order prepared exactly as requested. After she turned away from the table, an older waitress who had observed the exchange leaned down to the silent, red-faced girls and whispered with awe, "That's our Miss Lane. She's the owner's niece. Isn't she something?"

There were good times and bad, and through it all Bessie learned to hold on, to survive.

She met her handsome, kilted Scotsman at a church costume ball, where she was Miss Liberty. Bessie faced losing him when he enlisted in the army in World War I, but before he shipped overseas he proposed to her in an eleven-page letter. When he returned from the service, there were gentle days of courtship on the porch swing at 580 Laurel Avenue. When he left after their dates, he often met the local policeman walking the beat, who always asked, "And did you have a lovely evening?"

And David Jarvis always answered, "Yes, sir, lovely indeed."

On September 24, 1920, Bessie Lane married David Jarvis. She wore a stunning brown suit fashioned by Aunt Mame's dressmaker. It was trimmed around the bottom with fur and boasted a matching fur hat. Sixty years later, David and Bessie revisited 580 Laurel Avenue. Of course there'd been changes—and the porch swing was gone.

"I believe today is better, after all," Bessie ventured.

"Because of you, Dearie, because of you," David responded.

There were more times of survival. Their first home was one room with a shared bath, on the third floor of a house divided into apartments. Bessie cooked complete meals on a one-burner hot plate, juggling pans and dishes to get everything hot at the same time.

Bessie survived those pre-depression years when times were lean for her young family. She created a home in that little room, a haven her husband gratefully entered every evening, leaving the world outside. When their son, David, was born, Bessie negotiated for a larger apartment downstairs on the second floor. Six years later a daughter, Betty Lane, was born, and they found a house more suited to their growing family.

Bessie mothered not only her own little family but often found herself entertaining the neighborhood children. When a neighbor gave birth prematurely and couldn't cope, Bessie brought the baby into her own home and nurtured and loved her for weeks until the mother was strong again.

Several years later, when another neighbor needed to follow her husband in a job transfer, Bessie boldly offered $200 as a down payment on their house. The two women shook hands and settled the deal. Bessie had quite an announcement for Dave over dinner that evening.

After they moved to the new house just next door, their family was completed with the arrival of their third child. Big sister Betty named the baby Diane. Because of the fifteen-year span during which the children were born, Bessie found herself involved with children's activities for years: school programs and plays for which she sewed, reconstructing old dresses and coats into appropriate costumes; overseeing schoolwork and Sunday School lessons; singing and teaching her beloved old childhood songs to yet another generation; and baking the homemade after-school treats—cookies, doughnuts, or cream puffs—always making do with the limited resources available.

The onset of World War II demanded yet another kind of survival. There were sleepless nights of concern as her only son marched off to serve in his country's army. Those years took their toll, but Bessie survived. She survived the empty nest long before it became a "syndrome." She survived because she joyfully welcomed the new family members, the arrival of the grandchildren, one by one through the years. Bessie was born to be a grandmother, not only to her own five but to the children of friends and neighbors wherever she made her home.

"Of course, I'm not a bit proud of my grandchildren," she would say to any who would listen, beaming her approval like a benediction.

Bessie survived the loss of her beloved only son, not in that dreaded war but years later, when he was felled in the prime of life by a heart attack. Through the years, Bessie survived by looking ahead; there was always hope.

But hope faltered when Bessie lost her dear Dave after more than sixty years of marriage. Things had changed. Nothing was the same. Yet, a few years later, there was once again a glimmer of hope. Her first great-grandchild was on the way.

Bessie Lane Jarvis was gentle, but tough—a product of her history. She was a lady. She was a survivor.

But she never rocked that first great-grandchild.

After ninety-one years there was one
final thing Bessie could not survive.

4

In
the dead vast
and middle of the night

Distill'd
Almost to jelly
with the act of fear.

William Shakespeare
Hamlet

ONE

ONE NIGHT'S NIGHTMARE

⊰ The shrill ringing knifed through my sleep. I felt a sense of loss as I struggled to consciousness. I glanced at the clock on the bedside table. Eight o'clock. I had hoped for a leisurely Saturday morning with the paper and a cup of tea before getting out of bed.

"Hello."

"Mrs. Sandell?"

"Yes."

"This is the night supervisor at the nursing home."

"Yes" What now? I thought.

"I'm calling to tell you that your mother has unexplained bruises on her face."

"Oh?... And what have you done for her?"

"We've called the doctor and he has ordered X-rays."

"Please call me when the report gets back. In the meantime I'll get ready to come."

"All right. We'll call you."

"Thank you."

Well, there goes the quiet morning, I thought as I hurriedly made a cup of tea and began to dress. Though I was concerned about Mom, I wasn't terribly worried. She often bumped her legs or arms on the bed or the wheelchair. Her thin skin bruised easily. I was sure the nursing home was just being meticulous about reporting it to me.

At eight-thirty the phone rang again.

That's awfully fast, I thought as I answered.

"Mrs. Sandell?" It was the night supervisor again.

"Yes," I answered, pulling my car keys from my purse, ready to go.

"Are the reports back already?"

"No. But the aide has been suspended."

"I beg your pardon?" I tugged my earring off to hear her better.

"The aide has been suspended."

"What do you mean? Why didn't you say that on the first call? I'll be right there."

I hung up abruptly. My husband, Jim, laid down the morning paper and looked up at me questioningly.

"I don't know what's going on. I've got to get down there to see Mom. I'll call you from there."

"Just be careful," Jim said as he kissed me good-bye.

My stomach started to churn as I backed the car out of the driveway. Although it was Saturday morning, it seemed as if I hit every stoplight in the six miles between home and the nursing home.

Oh, Mom, what's going on? I replayed the two telephone calls over and over in my mind, trying to think what I had missed.

I tried to breathe deeply to calm myself, but with every block that last sentence repeated itself faster and faster: The aide has been suspended—the aide has been suspended—the aide has been suspended...

Finally I reached the last turn and then the driveway. Fortunately, at this time of morning there was no problem finding a parking space. I pushed through the wide entry door. The smell of breakfast permeated the halls, hitting my stomach sourly. My head was beginning to pound. I rushed down the hall, stopping at the door to her room. Inhaling deeply and putting a smile on my face, I stepped through the door.

I reeled as if I had been slapped! My stomach lurched. I thought I was going to be sick, but somehow I knew I had to retain control or I would faint.

There lay my darling little Mom, ninety-one years old, eighty-five pounds, upper body restrained in a posey (a vest-like garment used to restrain the wearer in bed or in a chair. See Appendix A). The top of her head was bruised and purpling. Her forehead was bruised. One temple was dark with the bluish imprint of a hand extending onto her cheek. Her nose was bloody and there was a blood clot under one eye.

"Mom!" I meant to say it gently. It came out as a shriek.

She opened her eyes and tried to reach her hand to mine.

"Here's my little honey," she said, her voice hardly more than a whisper.

I stepped closer and took her hand.

"Mom," I said, not knowing whether she would understand. "How did this happen? Who did this to you?"

She closed her eyes and shook her head—a wisp of movement.

"I don't know... she was big... I was scared."

"Who, Mom? Who was it? What did she look like?"

"So hard to tell." Every word seemed to take too much effort. "Sometime in the night," she sighed. "I'm so tired. I'm glad you're here, honey."

I leaned down to adjust the light blanket around her. Then I saw the ugly, dark bruises on her upper chest. I bit my lip to keep from crying out.

"You rest, Mom. I'll be right back."

In the hall I leaned against the wall for a minute, trying to regain what little composure I had left. I went to the nurses' desk, where there was a sudden spurt of activity with charts and files and papers and phones. No one would meet my eyes.

"I need to call Dr. Tynan. I want him to see Mother."

"Oh, we've talked with him, Mrs. Sandell," said a nurse. "The X-rays came back negative. Nothing's broken."

"I need to speak with him. What is his telephone number? I need it now, please."

The nurse knew I wouldn't be denied. She dialed the number without further comment and handed the phone to me. I was surprised that the doctor himself answered.

"Doctor, this is Diane Sandell. You are aware of what has happened to my mother, Bessie Jarvis. I need to have you see her today."

"I'm out on the road today, Mrs. Sandell. I don't know that I'll be able to make it."

"Doctor, if you do not see her today, I will have another physician see her. Today!"

I hung up and immediately dialed a family friend, a physician who had known Mother and tended her for years in the past. He said he'd come as soon as his office closed at noon.

An aide pushing an empty wheelchair stopped by my side and asked, "Do you know who did that to your mother?"

I told her how Mom had described the woman.

"Oh!" said the aide. "I'm not surprised." Then she went on with her errand.

Not surprised? I turned back to the desk; my head reeling with the overload of information I'd already taken in this morning.

"This thing obviously happened in the night. Why did you wait until eight before calling me? And why was I not told about the aide until a second call at 8:30?"

"It was reported at shift change, Mrs. Sandell, when the day shift was coming on. And we wanted to see that she was treated."

"You weren't up-front with me on that first call!"

As I spun away from the desk, it occurred to me that perhaps they wanted the aide off the premises before I arrived. It's probably a good thing I didn't see her face to face, I thought darkly, then realized I would like to have asked her, simply, "Why?"

With a start I realized I hadn't called Jim. I went down the hall to a pay phone away from the nurses' station. Jim answered on the first ring. After I explained, he said he'd call the children and then come down.

Then I called my friend Sue, who said, without hesitation, "I'll be right there. Oh, and, Diane, be sure to take pictures right away."

Another call home to ask Jim to bring the camera and film. Suddenly I realized I would have to call my sister, Betty Lane, in Pennsylvania. My fingers shook as I dialed her number. How could I tell her, from a public phone in the hall of a nursing home 3000 miles away, that our mother had been beaten in the night and that I had absolutely no answers?

While I was trying to choke it out, Betty Lane kept asking, "Shall I come? Do you want me to come now?"

We agreed it would be better for her to wait until we knew more about the situation. My mind kept crying, What more is there to know? It happened!

As I turned from the phone, one of the kitchen assistants asked if she could bring me something to drink, but past her shoulder I saw Sue hurrying down the hall toward me. I welcomed her hug, realizing I had dreaded going back into Mother's room alone.

While Sue and I stood by Mom's bed, waiting for Jim to arrive, the administrator of the nursing home came in with a nurse. She walked to the bed, glanced down at Mother, said brusquely, "That's too bad." Then she turned and strode out of the room without a glance in my direction or a word of explanation, apology, or comfort—literally without even acknowledging my presence. I was stunned.

Jim and our daughter Kathy arrived simultaneously, and there were all the explanations to go through again, retelling the little I knew, the incredibility of it all.

Sue urged me to take the pictures while we were still alone in the room. How could I take pictures of this obscenity committed against a woman to whom dignity was a way of life?

"You must!" Sue urged.

Kathy was stroking Mom's hands. She tried to smooth the ragged hair into a semblance of order. Mom had been so fastidious about her grooming. We couldn't even give her false teeth to her—they had been lost in the nursing home earlier.

My hands shook as I snapped several pictures.

"Kathy, please stay with Mom a while. I've got to get out of here. Sue, come walk with me?"

As we started down the hall, an aide fell into step with us and whispered as we walked.

"Mrs. Barton told me she heard what happened last night. She said to tell you she'd talk with you if you want. She's down in the activities room."

The aide turned down another hallway and Sue offered to go back to Mom's room.

"No, I want you with me. I need someone else to hear what she says, too."

We hurried to the activities room, and from the aide's description easily located her—a tiny, very frail, white-haired woman sitting by a window.

"Mrs. Barton?"

"Yes."

"I'm Diane Sandell, Bessie Jarvis's daughter. I understand you can tell me something about what happened to my mother last night."

Mrs. Barton glanced around the room, and I sensed her frailty and vulnerability.

"What can you tell me, Mrs. Barton?" I asked as gently as I could, afraid of having to believe whatever she might say.

"I know what time it was," she said with conviction. "I was awake. It happened twice, and I looked at the clock by my bed each time. It was at 11:30 last night, and again at one o'clock this morning."

Twice! I shuddered, seeing again those purple bruises that will remain forever in my memory, etched with the acid of horror, shock, and disbelief.

"I heard slapping sounds," Mrs. Barton went on, shivering, "and your mother yelled out, 'Please, don't hit me any more!' She said, 'What are you hitting me for?' And at one o'clock I heard her cry, 'Don't do that. It hurts. Please, don't hit me any more!'" Mrs. Barton covered her face with her hands.

"You're sure of the times?"

"Oh, yes. There was enough light from the hall to see. I didn't sleep after that."

"Thank you, Mrs. Barton." I saw again how very frail she was. She seemed to wilt before my eyes.

"I'm so sorry," she went on, fingering the edge of her lap robe with gnarled pale hands. "I should have called someone. I just couldn't. I'm so sorry."

I suddenly realized she was frightened for herself. My stomach lurched again. How many others might have heard? How many others might have been afraid to call for help? Why didn't any of the nurses hear, or the rest of the staff? If she was screaming, why did no one else hear? Why?

As we left the activities room, I found a nurse and asked her to check Mrs. Barton to make sure she was all right. I was concerned about leaving her there alone. When we got back to Mom's room, our son-in-law, Jim, a detective with a local police department, had arrived.

"What can I do, Mom?" he asked, giving me a hug.

"We need to call the police. Something awful is going on here."

"I'll do that for you," he said, immediately stepping into the hall.

"You're in official hands now," Sue said. "I'll go now before the police arrive. Call me later."

"I will, Sue. And thanks for coming. You'll never know how much you helped, just being here with me."

"I'll go now too," my husband said. "I'll take the film in for processing. Be back soon."

"The police are on the way," my son-in-law said as he came back into the room.

"I need to tell the administrator they're coming. I don't want them just coming through the doors."

"Shall I come along?" he offered, looking like my own personal knight in shining armor. I nodded gratefully.

I felt that people eyed us warily as we passed the nurses' station on the way to the administrator's office.

"I want to be up-front with you," I said as we met her in the hall. "We've called the police. They're on the way."

She merely nodded.

"By the way, I'd like to see Mother's records."

"I can't give you those."

"I need to see them. I need to know what happened."

"I can't let you see her records," she said, turning away.

"But I'm responsible for her."

"Sorry."

I turned away, vowing to myself that I would see Mom's records.

When the police arrived, I felt a sense of relief that it was now in their hands. They were very gentle with Mother and tried to ask her about what happened, but she couldn't give any real answer to their questions. By this time her fatigue was taking over. They took numerous photos of her injuries, and spoke with several people on the staff.

By the time they left, an aide had brought a lunch tray, but I didn't think Mom would be able to eat.

"I'm so sorry," the aide said, nodding toward Mom. "Of all people, not your mom. Couldn't I bring you some lunch too, or some tea?"

"Thank you, no, but could you bring some ice cream for Mother? I might be able to coax her to have some. I don't think she'll eat the lunch."

As I spooned softened ice cream for Mom, I thought of all the happy times we'd had ice cream together. I think she finally felt safer. She drifted off to sleep before she finished the dish.

"Now, you need to get out of here for a while," my husband said, reappearing after his errand.

"Oh, I can't."

"You can and will," he insisted, urging me gently toward the door. "She'll sleep awhile. We'll come right back. She'll be all right. You need to sit and have a cup of tea."

It was true. I was mentally and physically exhausted. When we got to the car, the first real tears came. And came, and came. When they seemed to be over, we drove to a nearby coffee shop and ordered tea and toast. I couldn't face anything else.

"What are we going to do, Jim?"

"You are going to drink your tea."

"We've got to get her out of there."

"Yes, but don't try to solve that now."

"We've got to."

"Come on, now, have your tea. You've got to regroup. You've got to stay strong for her. You know they'll watch her extra carefully now.

We'll handle the other things one by one."

I knew he was right but I still couldn't focus. I had to get back to the nursing home.

The afternoon wore on. Our other two children came and went. We told the story again and again. It didn't get any easier.

Our friend Dr. Nichols came and examined Mother with shocked disbelief. He checked the medical records; though he was appalled with the situation, he felt she would recover from the physical injuries, but was concerned about the potential emotional aftermath of her ordeal. I knew I could trust him, so my concerns about her immediate physical condition were alleviated.

Still, walking out the door to go home that evening was one of the hardest things I have ever had to do. Although Mother was sleeping peacefully as we tiptoed from her room, I knew it would be a long, sleepless night for me.

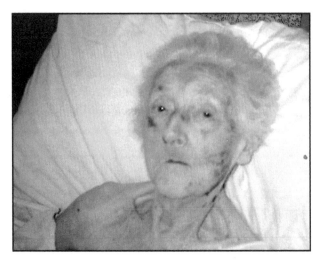

BESSIE JARVIS—THE MORNING AFTER

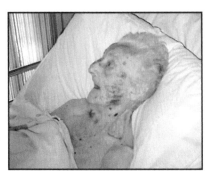

"Here's my little honey…"
Black and blue and
bloodied—wondering why

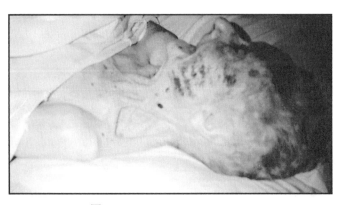

THE TELL-TALE HANDPRINT

"Missus Jarbits?"

The tiny tow-headed boy
held out a grubby fist full
of violets and lilies of the valley,
clods of dirt clinging to thready roots,
trickling down his shirt front.

"I brought you flowers."

"And how gorgeous they are,"
Bessie said, recognizing the blossoms from her
own flower bed behind the house.

"Thank you for your kindness, young sir.
I think I might find a cookie in my pantry.
Would you like to come help me look?"

"Oh, yes!" The boy beamed.
"Could I have one for
each hand,
please?"

Two

Turn Around, Turn Around

⊰ Sunday dawned bright and hot, a typical California July day, but my spirit was February frozen. I had been wakeful all night, asking the same questions over and over, replaying all the events of the previous day. Something twisted and curled beneath my consciousness, keeping me uneasy even though Jim repeatedly assured me that the staff would be extra watchful.

Suddenly it hit me: The aide had been suspended. But what if she hadn't done it? What if it had been someone else?

"We've got to get her out of there," I announced as if it were a new thought. I pulled on a cool outfit and ran a brush through my hair. "I've got to get over there now."

"Do you want me to come?" Jim asked, draining his coffee mug.

"Not this time. I'll be all right. You get some rest. You've got to go back to work tomorrow."

Once again I was hurrying over the few miles to the nursing home, my thoughts careening back twenty-five years to the crises that brought Mom and Dad into our home for the remainder of their lives.

It had been a perfect, calendar-picture "White Christmas" day in Bowie, Maryland, back in 1961, but it wasn't ideal logistically. Mom was in the hospital, recovering from gall bladder surgery, and Dad stayed in Baltimore to visit her. He planned to come the next day. Jim's parents came out from Baltimore and helped us celebrate merrily with our two-year-old, Kathy. We were determined not to let undue concern about Mom's hospitalization dampen our toddler's Christmas. We were looking forward to having Jim's mother stay and visit with us that week while his dad went back to work.

⚜

A red light stopped me at the last intersection before the nursing home, and I chuckled mirthlessly, remembering that another early morning telephone call had shattered our peace that morning after Christmas so many years ago.

"Good morning, Diane. It's Dave."

"Hi, big brother. Did you have a merry Christmas?"

"Well, yes, but that's not why I'm calling. Dad was in an accident last night. He's in the hospital."

"What happened?" Fear slithered in beneath Dave's calm tone of voice.

"We felt you didn't need to come. I knew you were coming today to see Mom."

"Dave, tell me what happened."

"He was on the way home from visiting Mom—nearly home in fact—when a tractor-trailer truck skidded on the ice and broadsided his car."

"Bro—ther!" I shrieked the nickname, waiting for the worst.

"It's all right, Di. He's going to be all right. You can swing by the hospital to see for yourself when you come see Mom later. It's strange isn't it, having your parents in two different hospitals at Christmas?"

The minute Dave hung up, I dialed my best friend in Baltimore—the one who would tell me what hung in the air, unspoken, under Dave's brisk assurance.

"Patty, it's Di. I've got to ask you to do something for me right away and call me back."

"Sure, Diane. What's up?"

I told her the facts I knew as quickly as possible and asked her to confirm Dad's condition and call me right back. Then I waited, my hand on the receiver. I answered on the first ring fifteen long minutes later.

"It's quite a story, Di. I called the hospital, and then your folks' neighbor, Mrs. Curry. She drove by the accident right after it happened and recognized his car. She knew your mom was in the hospital, so she went to the hospital with him. His condition is critical."

"I knew Dave wasn't telling me everything. What happened?"

"As I said, Mrs. Curry came by right after the accident happened. She went to the hospital with him. He seemed okay, and she was going to drive him home. The hospital examined him and released him, but he fainted in the lobby on the way out. They admitted him for observation and found internal bleeding. They won't know anything for sure till tests come back today. Mrs. Curry called Dave and he came in."

"Thanks, Patty. I knew you'd level with me. Dave is so darned protective. I'm coming in. I don't know how yet, but I'll get there."

⁓⁂⁓

In the hot July sunshine, I shivered, remembering the funny, unfunny trip into Baltimore on snowy streets that day after Christmas, slipping and sliding in my neighbor's Volkswagen bug. Barbara was at the wheel, her two children with Grandma Sandell in the backseat, holding Kathy on her lap, with me, pregnant in the other front seat.

Mom Sandell offered to watch Kathy till we knew what the situation was, so Barbara dropped me off at the hospital and took them on to Sandells' home.

It surprised me to find Dad looking okay, but apologetic.

"Oh, honey, you shouldn't have come. I'll be okay. I know the roads are... "

"Dad, of course I had to come."

"But who's watching the baby? How did you get here? Surely you didn't drive. Where's Jim?"

"Slow down, Dad. Everything's under control," I lied, feeling very much not under control. "Mom Sandell has Kathy, and Jim will be here later."

I realized Jim had gone to work this morning before Dave called. He didn't know what was going on, or even where I was. I'd have to call him as soon as possible.

I learned that Dad's injuries were internal. The doctor suspected the spleen was leaking blood. Dad would need to be hospitalized until they could determine whether the injury would heal itself or if he'd need surgery.

Because the weather was so bad, the Sandells insisted we all stay with them for the duration. When I reached Jim at work, he agreed to pick up things we would need from home and secure the house. We stayed ten days in Baltimore. Dad was obsessive about my driving in the weather, so I assured him I'd take the bus to the hospital, and that I'd wait for Jim to get home from work at night before trying to go see Mother in another hospital on the far side of town. It was a tense time, juggling the needs of each parent, protecting each from worry about the other.

It turned out that Mom was released before Dad. With both parents being released from different hospitals, and neither able to care for the other, we brought them both into our guestroom in Bowie to recuperate. When we recognized they would need to live closer to family, we faced the painful task of dismantling their home in Baltimore, the house Mom bought from a neighbor on the spur of the moment with a $200 down payment, the house where I was born and lived for twenty-one years till I married Jim, the house of a million memories.

We found a little apartment near us and moved their furniture and belongings, and when Mom and Dad seemed well enough, moved them into their new nest. It didn't work. Because of his injuries, Dad couldn't go back to work, and had to retire. Mom was having fainting spells. Dad couldn't cope. After several middle-of-the-night rescue trips, two-year-old in tow, we came to the conclusion that if we were to be on twenty-four-hour call it would be easier for all of us to be living under one roof.

Once again we found ourselves packing cartons and crates with years of memories: family photo albums, a potholder I wove in second grade, Mom's cut glass vase, and her beloved dark brown chiffon dancing dress (long outgrown, but my sister Betty Lane had modeled it at Mom and Dad's fortieth wedding anniversary two years before).

BESSIE AND DAVID JARVIS, IN HAPPIER TIMES

We squeezed and stretched and created a nest for five, knowing we'd be six before many months, when our new baby would arrive. As Mom and Dad got stronger and more confident in their new surroundings and status, they became a great team. They were there to help run the household, having pet projects they each enjoyed. Mom's fried chicken and potato salad became legendary and I looked forward to her night to cook. Dad became active in our brand-new little church. They had a new sense of security, and we had the support of live-in grandparents. We were quite a family, and a few months later our son, Mark, made his entrance on the scene.

Mom loved being Granny. She had a gift with newborns, singing and rocking and loving both the baby and the toddler. The arrangement worked so well that four years later, when Jim was transferred to Cleveland, they came along with us. Two years later we all sang "California, here we come," traveling across the country when we were transferred to Southern California. Our family grew to seven in 1969, when our youngest daughter, Kim, was born.

But we weren't finished moving. We were sent to Schenectady, New York for six years before we finally made our last move back to California. With each move it seemed as if our entourage was growing and changing, but Granny and Grandpop, as they became known, were a given constant.

On every street where we lived, Mom became the Granny of all, both kids and parents. She had only to look at a tiny young face and she'd be reaching out her arms for a hug. Hugs were always rewarded with goodies—often her favorite cake-like chocolate drop cookies, doubly good with fudgey mocha frosting, kept in abundant supply in the old starburst cookie tin on the second shelf.

"One for each hand," she'd croon, her face wreathed with indulgent smiles. That was her motto, quickly adopted by all the grandchildren and all the neighborhood kids as well. Maybe some adults, too!

And now these arms that had reached out for hugs and offered love and cookies had tried, without success, to fend off hostile arms that had beaten her mercilessly.

Don't worry, Mom, I breathed silently as I parked the car and hurried through the nursing home door. You're moving again, Mom. We'll get you out of here.

After checking to see that Mother was all right, I went to the nurses' station. I knew it would take me a while to find a new facility, but I needed reassurance about her care and condition until that time. One of the aides who had been especially nice, keeping Mom's hair groomed the way she liked it, seeing that she was well dressed, and putting her jewelry on, had been transferred to a beautiful new wing. I would feel safer if I could get Mom into her care again.

"I'd like to have Mother moved to the new wing," I said to the nurse at the desk.

"We can't move her there, Mrs. Sandell," she replied.

"She's got to be moved!" My voice rose several pitches as tension strangled me. "No one heard her screaming the other night. You've got to move her where she'll be under better observation."

"Well, there is an opening across the hall from the nurses' station—right over there. I think we could probably arrange to have her moved there."

"Please see to it as soon as possible."

As I left the facility, I rested my head on the steering wheel and let new tears of frustration come. Besides the physical weariness from lack of sleep, I was mentally exhausted as well.

I scanned the short list of the facilities I'd visited before placing Mom here, and wondered where to begin. I had chosen this nursing home with extreme care as the best available at the time we placed her here three years before. I quickly scratched several off the list. Having seen them, I knew they were unacceptable. From the remaining names a route slowly emerged and I began a traumatic journey.

I knew I was being paranoid, but I saw problems on every side. This one smelled, that one was dark, in another one the residents were listless, in another the personnel unresponsive. But in addition to my requirements, there were other factors—the availability of space at all, and the fact that Mother would have to be a partial-pay resident (in California, Medi-Cal; other states, Medicaid), for whom there were limited spaces. And finally, the personnel I spoke with seemed hesitant to talk with me after I told them Mother had been beaten, and described the condition she was in.

"That was the hardest to take," I complained to Jim later that evening when I was reporting my lack of success. "Why wouldn't they help? Don't they care? They're supposed to be care facilities."

"They haven't seen her," Jim said with his usual calm. "They don't know the story; they're probably afraid you're exaggerating and will be paranoid about anything they do."

"Yes, I probably will," I responded, not realizing he was gently teasing me.

"Now, you can't do any more tonight. Try to get some rest."

"Do you realize how many times you've said that to me these past two days?" I laughed finally, though weakly, and took his extended hand.

When sorrows come,
they come not in single spies,
But in battalions

William Shakespeare

Hamlet

The worst is not
So long as we can say,
"This is the worst."

William Shakespeare

King Lear

THREE

GET THE HELL OUT OF DODGE

⊰ Monday morning called the rest of the family back
to their jobs, and I had a hollow sense of "business as usual," for which
I wasn't ready. Even the halls of the nursing home were bustling with
normal activity, as if nothing had happened.

"Oh, Mrs. Sandell," the nurse at the station called out a little too
breezily. "Dr. Buford examined your mother yesterday. He says she's
doing fine."

"Dr. Buford! I told Dr. Tynan I'd have my own physician examine
her Saturday. Why didn't you call to let me know?"

"We knew you wanted her seen."

"I wanted her seen Saturday. I had her examined Saturday. She
shouldn't have had to go through it again with another doctor, as
frightened as she is. I should have been here with her! You should
have called me!"

I hurried down the hall and found Mother very shrunken and quiet,
her searching, fearful eyes the most active thing about her. How could
I reassure her when I had no control over who came and went, or
what they might think it necessary to do to her? How could I protect
this wounded little child? After sitting with her for an hour, just speaking quietly to her, stroking her hand, reassuring myself that she was
all right, I slipped out as she dozed.

I drove to the photo lab and picked up the pictures Jim had left on
Saturday. I hurried back to the car and tore open the envelope. As
awful as it had been to see her bruises on Saturday, I wasn't prepared
for the stunning graphic reality of the pictures. While I could mentally shut out some of the horror the other day by focusing on other

29

things in the room, the stark images frozen in the still frames would not allow such diversion. The bruises riveted my attention; they were worse than I had even dreamed that long sleepless weekend. A cold rage began to coil in my stomach, numbing my senses.

I don't remember going home or calling Jim about the pictures, or picking up Kim, our eighteen-year-old daughter, who went back to the nursing home with me. The pictures of the bruises superimposed themselves on everything I saw, and seemed to pulse with the throbbing of my head. When Dr. Tynan came in later, his first visit since the beating, I looked at him as if at a stranger. He leaned down to look at Mother's face.

"That could have happened in a fall," he said, pointing to the bruise on her forehead.

"And that one could have happened when they picked her up."

On the verge of hysteria, I almost laughed. They pick them up by their faces?

"No, Doctor," Kim interrupted emphatically. "She was beaten."

He didn't respond. I knew then that even though she was listed as his patient, he wasn't involved—didn't want to be involved. But what did it matter, I thought coldly, she won't be here that much longer.

The days that followed are a blur. I toured facilities in the mornings, but found none acceptable. Frustrated, I would come home and do the necessary mundane chores. I laundered and mended all Mother's clothing, preparing for the move. I shopped for new things she needed, brought them home and marked them with her name, experiencing déjà vu from when the children were little and I did the same things for their school clothes. Each time I visited Mom (at least twice a day) she seemed quieter and more withdrawn, curling into a fetal position like a shriveling flower. Seeing her like that, it became harder and harder to go in, and every time I went through the nursing home doors I felt I was "on display."

Even though I knew we'd be moving Mother as soon as I could find a place for her, I was not satisfied to leave things as they were with Dr. Tynan. I felt he had let Mother down and us as well. For the first time,

I began to understand that we had the right to certain expectations of a physician, even though he was under the umbrella of the facility provision. When I called to ask for an appointment, he immediately offered to withdraw from the case.

Remember, always be a lady. "No, Doctor, I have not made that decision yet. I need to talk with you. May I come to your office?"

"No," he countered quickly. "I see patients there."

Of course you see patients there... I wondered what difference that made... remember, a lady.... "Then where could we meet, and when?" I asked.

"How about the hospital in the morning—about eight o'clock?"

"Fine. I'll be there."

At the hospital the next morning, when Doctor Tynan answered the page and came to the lobby, I asked if we could speak somewhere privately. He nodded at the big glass doors and steered me out onto the sidewalk. I had hoped for a more businesslike atmosphere—a desk, an office, a conference room—but so be it.

Always be a lady.

"Dr. Tynan, thank you for seeing me. I just needed to let you know, in person, that I am very disappointed in your handling of this case. With the severity of my mother's beatings last Friday night, I felt you should have been there for her, and for the rest of us as the family of your patient. She needed a physician she could trust to care about what happened to her. We did too, but we didn't get it."

When I had finished, Dr. Tynan just looked at me. I think he was surprised there wasn't more. Finally he said, "I'm sorry I disappointed you." Then he turned and went back into the hospital. That was all.

Two days later I wrote to tell him we would no longer need his services. I didn't ask for another doctor at the nursing home because I knew Mother would be leaving soon.

By Friday, two weeks after the beatings, I was no closer to finding a new facility, and was running out of possibilities as well as hope. I had visited all the homes on my list, and some that weren't, but could not bring myself to choose. Finally, through a friend, I was given the phone number of a facility I hadn't previously heard of. It came highly recommended. I started to pocket the number. I'll call Monday, I thought, too tired to deal with yet another disappointment. But my friend wouldn't let it go. I threw up every excuse I could think of, and she shot them all down.

"They might not even have a bed open," I finished lamely.

"But they just might," she retorted, handing me the phone.

And they did. And even though it was late Friday afternoon, and the facility was on the far side of the county, I went to look at it.

Meg Stuckey, the director of admissions I had spoken with, met me at the door and showed me into her office, indicating a chair as she sat down at the desk. There was a soothing, unhurried cordiality about her. I immediately felt at ease.

"As I told you on the phone, I need a bed for my mother," I began, and told her the whole story. As I finished, I drew the pictures from my purse and showed them to her. Her face registered her reaction.

"We do have a bed," she said quietly, but firmly, "and we'll be glad to accept her. Let me show you around."

There was an atmosphere about the place that instilled comfort and confidence. I finally felt secure.

"When can I bring her?" I asked as we returned to Meg's office. I would have been willing to bring her that very hour.

"Well, it's Friday evening. I'd like to have full staff on duty so we can make the transition as easy as possible for your mother. How about Monday morning between ten and eleven?"

It was settled. For the first time since the incident, I slept well, knowing that finally there was an end in sight.

Saturday morning I was optimistic and cheerful as I called the nursing home. After identifying myself to the desk nurse, I told her of my plans to move Mother on Monday morning, and asked that she start whatever checkout procedures were necessary.

"And would you order an ambulance for ten o'clock, please. We'll be ready by then."

"I'll see to it, Mrs. Sandell."

"I'll be in and out today and tomorrow, packing Mother's things." We spent the weekend visiting with Mom and boxing up her clothing and costume jewelry, the framed family pictures she kept on the dresser, a stuffed animal or two that Kim had given her, the tin box of Hershey bars she kept to share with the aides in happier days. I couldn't tell if Mom really understood what was happening. I kept up a steady chatter about other moves we'd made together, but Mom was very quiet. Whenever anyone came into the room, she seemed to shrivel.

Monday morning I was awake before dawn, but I knew there was no reason to get there too early. The ambulance wasn't scheduled until ten. Although I had been sleeping better, I was still churned up about actually getting Mom out of there. Kim was going to come with me to help, and she was eager to get going too. We decided to take two cars in case the boxes wouldn't all fit in mine.

We arrived for the last time, I thought, grimly, about nine o'clock. I was surprised, but relieved, to see Mother dressed and ready, waiting in a wheelchair. She was wearing a pale blue flowered muumuu and a thin white sweater. She already had a lap robe tucked around her legs. Kim and I loaded the boxes into her car and came back to wait for the ambulance. I brushed Mother's hair. I wanted her to look nice for her ride. When I realized it was nearly ten, I went to see if the ambulance had arrived.

"What time did the ambulance company say they'd be here?" I asked the nurse. "We asked for ten o'clock."

"Just a minute, I'll check." She pulled Mother's file. "No ambulance was ordered, Mrs. Sandell."

"I spoke with the desk nurse Saturday morning, and specifically requested an ambulance. I was told it would be taken care of."

"I'll check and see what they can do."

I went to Mother's room to wait once more. "Do you think, just once," I asked Kim with a sigh, "things could go right?"

"Nope!" Kim answered with a little giggle, trying to lift my spirits. "That would be too easy."

"Mrs. Sandell," the nurse said at the door of the room, "since it

33

wasn't pre-ordered the ambulance will take about an hour and a half. Oh, and the cost will be two hundred dollars."

Kim's look said Nope; it won't be easy, only this time she wasn't giggling.

"Forget it!" I said abruptly to the nurse. "We can't wait any longer. We'll take her ourselves." What I really wanted to say was, I just want to get the hell out of Dodge, an old family joke about escaping unpleasantness. But that didn't fit Mother's picture of a lady. I didn't feel much like Mother's picture of a lady.

Kim and I wheeled Mom out to my car and struggled to get this tiny shriveled woman into the front seat. I had brought pillows to cushion her in the ambulance, so I plumped them all around her, forming a padded nest. I tucked the lap robe around her knees and finally brought the seat belt across her lap and shoulders.

I locked the car door and turned to speak to Kim about the streets we'd take to the new facility. An aide had come out to pick up the wheelchair. She looked at me blankly.

"You know," she said sullenly, "we really did take very good care of her here."

Fly
little birdies;
fly around the ring
Fly little birdies while we all sing.
Then fly down at some child's feet
And I'll sing you a song so soft and sweet.

Rest little birdies; yes rest awhile
Then go on to another child,
Then fly down at some child's feet
And I'll sing you a song
so soft and
sweet.

Author unknown

Four

Over the River and Through the Woods

⌁ I was aware of Kim's hand on my arm, her eyes wide and dark as she watched the aide disappear through the nursing home door.

"Come on, Mom, let's just get out of here."

"Kim, I'm just about undone. You follow me. I'll go slow and stay in the right lane. If you see me doing something silly or driving erratically, honk the horn at me. We'll stop if we have to."

"Okay, Mom. We'll get there. Let's go."

We pulled out of the parking lot in tandem. I drove with my left hand, the right thrown across Mother's chest as I used to do with the kids before seat belts. She became agitated; flailing her arms and hands. I tried to hold her hand and stroke it without taking my eyes off the road.

"Remember how we used to take rides, Mom?" It occurred to me that this could well be Mother's last car ride. Tears blurred my vision. "And we'd laugh and sing," I said as gaily as I could. "Let's sing, Mom."

"Over the river and through the woods, to Grandmother's house we go...."

Maybe not the best choice of songs. "You're going to have a new house, Mom—Granny. Won't that be great? You'll like it there. Things will be all right now." I realized I was praying that they would.

"Down beside the beautiful sea, that's where the children love to be...."

"Remember how you liked to go to the seashore in Maryland, Mom? We'd sing all the way. Come on, Mom, sing with me..."

"I think when I read that sweet story of old, when Jesus was here among men, how He called little children as lambs to His fold, I should like to have been with Him then."

"Come on, Mom, next verse."

Always songs about children. She loved the little ones so. An urgent honking startled me. I glanced in the rearview mirror and saw Kim motioning me forward. I wondered how long the traffic signal had been green. At least Mother was calmer now.

"Fly little birdies, fly around the ring, fly little birdies while we all sing..."

Finally we arrived at the new facility. I felt as if I had pushed the car the whole ten miles. I was exhausted. My face was a mess. I'd been crying and I needed to blow my nose! I mopped my face with a tissue and went inside.

"We've been expecting you," Meg Stuckey greeted me, aware of my face. "Bring your car right around by the side door and I'll have someone meet you. Her room is ready."

Soon Mother was tucked into her new surroundings. Worn out from all the activity, she fell asleep. Kim and I straightened things in her new drawers, and sat by her bed most of the afternoon. Every time Mom stirred, I'd reassure her she was in her nice new home.

In the next two weeks I saw how dedicated and caring the new facility really was. Recognizing her fear, the director of nursing asked the entire staff to cooperate in a program to instill trust again. She requested that everyone who passed Mother's door take a moment to look in and call out 'Hello' and call her by name; however, no one was to go near her bed or touch her except the aides and nurses who cared for her needs. Because of her many bruises, and her increasing lack of movement, a special bed with a heated water mattress was ordered. This was very soothing to her; she would lie on her side and stroke the mattress, feeling the water move beneath her fingers.

I brought fresh flowers and candy nearly every day—both treats she had enjoyed so much in the past. She seemed unresponsive. Sometimes she asked me where her mother was; sometimes she called me

"Mother," or "Sister." Thinking it would help her regain a sense of reality I sometimes tried to correct her by telling her who I was, but that often agitated her. If she seemed more peaceful calling me "Mother," why not?

But through all this I could see that her bruises were healing, and I hoped her psyche was, as well. I couldn't help but notice the irony. Mother often had bruises on her arms and legs at the old nursing home, and the reasonable-sounding explanation was that the elderly have such fragile skin it sometimes bruises, even in the necessary frequent turning of the person in bed. It was also suggested that they even accidentally bruise themselves moving about. This can be true, yet Mother had been here only two weeks and the marks on her body were nearly gone, though she was being handled and turned even more frequently because of her diminished capacity to turn herself. Yet there was no new bruising.

It wasn't all perfect: fear injected itself once again when the administrator told me Mother had been yelling a lot, especially at night, and that she was disturbing other residents. I felt as if I'd been called to the principal's office.

"If she continues being noisy will you have to move her to another facility?" I asked. I'm not sure how I knew that could be a possibility.

"Not at this time, Mrs. Sandell."

I was not reassured. "If it comes to that, where would you move her?"

"It's possible she might have to go to a secured facility."

I shuddered. "Secured" was a euphemism for "locked." I had seen some locked facilities. I couldn't face that possibility. It didn't occur to me to ask why my mother, who couldn't walk or even get out of bed, would need to be in a locked facility.

I knew she had been noisy at the previous nursing home. She would call out or clap her hands as loudly as she could when nobody responded to her need for the bathroom. She often had accidents while waiting for assistance. She was even considered combative, but I was learning that perhaps there were valid reasons. Her most basic needs were being ignored because she was considered "difficult," and this was an affront to her dignity. And finally, she had been fighting for her life. Maybe more than once. No amount of noisiness or combativeness excused the lack of care or the beatings that occurred in the nursing home that had contracted to care for her.

I felt my irritation and frustration rising again. I knew the administrator needed to see the pictures. I brought them from home later that day. As he looked at them silently, his somber face reflected his new understanding of what she had been through. There was no further talk of moving her.

It was getting harder and harder to visit Mom. She was increasingly unaware and unresponsive, sleeping most of the time and confused when she was awake. Still, I'd try to visit with her as if she understood every word. It was taking a toll on me. One Thursday, several weeks after we'd transferred her, I walked into her room with a heavy heart.

"Here's my honey, Di!" exclaimed the wraith-like figure in the bed.

"Mom!" I cried, rushing to give her a kiss, trying not to be too vigorous in hugging her. She clung to my hand as if she'd just returned from a long, long trip—and maybe she had. "Have you had lunch, Mom?" I was always aware of trying to get food into her. "How about some ice cream?"

"Are we celebrating, Honey?" Mom's eyes were sparkling.

"Absolutely! Would you like to have a birthday party, Mother?"

"With strawberry ice cream?"

"With strawberry ice cream!" My throat was tight and my eyes filled with tears. I stumbled into the hall and stopped the first aide I saw.

"Please," I said, as if grasping for a lifeline. "I need a dish of strawberry ice cream. Right now! Please!" She must have understood my SOS, for within minutes she brought a large sundae dish full of beautiful strawberry ice cream.

I laughed and cried as I spooned mouthful after mouthful into Mother's eager lips. And we sang! I sang "Happy Birthday" to her, and she sang it to me. We sang all her old favorites, even Christmas carols.

She ate the whole dish of ice cream.

"What a party," she smiled contentedly. "Thanks, Honey."

Weary from the exertion, she soon drifted to sleep and I went home, drained but happy.

I was eager to see her the next day to see if the new alertness was holding. I arrived early, bringing flowers and candy and the latest letter from Betty Lane, but Mom was asleep when I got there and didn't respond to my quiet attempts to wake her. I left about four in the afternoon, disappointed and dispirited. Jim was quick to recognize my emptiness and offered to postpone our scheduled dinner out with Kim, but I thought we all might benefit from being waited upon and cared for.

It was a lovely evening. We found lots to talk about and it seemed good to just relax and enjoy one another, making plans for a cruise we three had promised ourselves at Christmas time. We laughed a lot, though quietly.

When we got home at nine o'clock, the phone was ringing.

Mother had just passed away.

My Mom is very special, God, hear my whispered prayer,
I miss her very much You know There's sadness everywhere.

"I know, I know my child, I'll wipe away your tears.
It's time for her to be with Me, You've had her many years.
She's oh, so happy home with Me, My special loving guest,
She wanted Peace and Comfort,
and Oh yes, some needed rest.
Diane, your Mom is singing, Her voice raised up in praise,
Your Dad was there to greet her,
They're together all the days.
Your Mom and Dad are with Me in everything they do, and
We'll be here—We Promise
When your life on earth is through."

Oh Lord, I feel much better, and I love You very much,
I need You close beside me, I need Your loving touch.
I Miss her, so my tears will flow—

"I know—it's good to cry, I'll stay close by and hold you
And pat each teardrop dry."

Ann Simons
For Bessie Jarvis
1988

FIVE

5/3 TURKEY

⌦ Are we ever really ready to say good-bye to a parent? Even if they've been very ill; even if they've become someone we don't know; even if their "quality of life" has no quality as we see it; are we ever really ready to say good-bye? Jim's parents were both gone; my dad had died four years before; now Mom. All of our parents' generation was now gone. Even though I had been her "parent" much of these last few months, suddenly I felt very alone. My roots were gone. And yet I felt relief, and then guilt for the relief. It took me a long time to realize both feelings were natural. I was relieved that her struggles were over. I thought, wrongly, that mine were too.

"Remember, Diane, always be a lady."

"Turkey," Jim used to call her, teasing.

"You're the turkey," she'd give right back to him. She'd adored him from the time he was fifteen years old.

When we arrived at the new facility, we were told Mother had awakened after I left at four, and had eaten a very good dinner.

No more of Mom's potato salad. No more homemade cream puffs or doughnuts. No more Ladies' Aid Cake (see Appendix K) or chocolate drop cookies.

But she'd had a good meal. That's good, I thought. She always insisted on a good meal before leaving on a trip.

They had found her, peacefully gone, at bedtime rounds.

I wept, wishing I'd been there when she woke up that afternoon.

"Never forget, a lady always carries a freshly pressed handkerchief."

But I was grateful for the wonderful day before, when we'd had ice cream and birthday songs.

One of her favorite birthday presents when she was a little girl was a white kitten she'd named Tissue Baby.

"I'm just thankful," I said to Jim and Kim, "that the bruises are all healed. There's not a mark on her now."

"Why did it have to happen to her?" Kim asked, knowing there wasn't an answer.

When she went into the other nursing home, she was Bess Jarvis, a lady. They turned her into someone else. The new facility had given her back to us as much as they were able.

Mark arrived, looking frustrated and angry by the news as much as saddened. His wife, Dorie, just a few weeks from delivering Granny's first great-grandchild, was home resting.

"Remember, Mark," Granny used to say, "I've loved you since I held you as a baby in my arms. Grandma will never stop loving her boy."

I had called our other daughter, Kathy, and her husband, who were out of town on vacation. They'd return in the morning.

The mortuary assistant appeared discreetly at the doorway. The others rose to leave the room.

"I'll stay," I said, holding Mother's hand.

Now I lay me down to sleep—

"It may be difficult for you," he said.

I pray the Lord my soul to keep—

"I need to be with her, especially now."

If I should die before I—

How many times had she prayed so with my children, treasuring their tiny folded hands, the eyes that sometimes peeked from between their fingers?

I knew there would be a zippered body bag, but for some reason the rubber gloves shocked me more, stabbing at my injured heart.

I pray the Lord, my soul to take.

"You will be very gentle with her," I said with pleading in my voice.

Down beside the beautiful sea, that's where the children love to be—

"Yes, of course I will."

"That is to go along with her," I said, nodding at the soft new teddy bear Kim had tucked in her arm.

Building sand castles on the shore and listening to the breakers roar—

"Certainly." He smiled as if every ninety-one-year-old lady made her final ride with a new teddy in her arms. "I need to close now, if you want to step out."

"No, I'll stay." I patted Mother's arm one more time before he zipped the bag shut. "Just be very gentle with her, please."

Good-bye, Mom…

I walked with him to the same side door where we'd brought Mother in four weeks earlier. The others were waiting for me there. When the hearse started to pull away, the attendant rolled down the window.

I come to the garden alone…

"I will be very careful with her, Mrs. Sandell."

Good-bye, Mother… good-bye… 5/3….

Mother had chosen to be cremated, as had Dad several years before. It was no easier this time, but at least I knew what to do, what to expect. We had chosen aerial distribution of the ashes over the ocean, and on the appointed morning, Jim and I drove to Newport Beach, where we parked above the sand near the pier. The pilot had told us he would buzz the pier twice, parallel to the shoreline, then circle around and fly straight out over the pier into the horizon to the three-mile limit before scattering the ashes.

"She's on her way to Pop," I said, clinging tightly to Jim's arm as the little plane shot, arrow-straight, over the pier into the bright shimmering autumn light above the waves. We dropped a yellow rose into the water and watched it float for a moment.

"She's at peace now. No more hurts. No more tears. Good-bye, Mom."

Good-bye, Mother… good-bye.

It was going to be all right. The healing had begun.

When we got back to the car, I couldn't help giggling. Jim glanced at me warily, suspecting hysteria, but I explained.

"Remember the parking ticket Betty Lane and I got when we came

45

here for Dad? We were running late and were afraid we'd miss seeing the plane. I put money in the meter, but didn't notice it was for
the stall next to us. I can just hear Dad teasing, "At least you didn't
get a ticket this time. Of course, that's probably because Jim's here to
handle it this time.'"

"It's good to hear you laughing," Jim said. "Let's don't go yet. Let's
have lunch."

Jim has always known how therapeutic the ocean is for me. The
salt air, the breezes, and the murmur of the water are better for me
than medicine. We found a restaurant with outdoor tables, boats
docked right alongside, and had a fine seafood luncheon. We toasted
Mom with a glass of white wine.

Good-bye, Mother...5/3...

A few weeks later, when Betty Lane was able to arrange a week off
from her teaching position, she came from Pennsylvania, and we
had a memorial service celebrating Mom's life. It gave not only her
family, but her adopted "family" of friends and neighbors who had
gone through this trauma with us, an opportunity to reclaim the
happy memories, the real person behind the battered shell we'd seen
at the last.

...Thornton Wilder said, "The highest tribute to the dead is
not grief but gratitude." We're thankful for all our memories
of Granny Jarvis...

...that look we shared when we were both "being ornery"
—then a smile—then laughter...Grandma always saw good and
humor in everything...Grandma, not the kids, was always
the first one up on Christmas or Easter mornings, waking
us all with the call that Santa or the Easter Bunny had come...

...singing all the songs...playing cards...anticipation and
excitement...the secret Granny-code "5/3"...

...the delicate things—yellow roses, birds, beautiful
fragrances, peaceful walks, holding babies...

...gift envelopes with a Granny kitty and a baby kitty in front of a
line drawing house, smoke coming out of the chimney, flowers

all around—and inside the envelope a crisp new dollar bill…
and of course, ✕ ✕ ✕, ⭕ ⭕ ⭕…5/3…
…lilies of the valley…Christmas…Grandpa putting the hooks
in all the ornaments, Granny by his side, diligently supervising
where we were to hang each ornament on the tree…
…yellow roses…Now I lay me down to sleep…
…Granny, I'll always remember…
…Of course, I'm not very proud of them…of course,
I don't love them very much…
And don't forget…always be a lady…

⚜

It was a warm and moving memorial service. We sang all her favorite hymns: How Great Thou Art; It Is Well With My Soul; In The Garden; and even Jesus Loves Me, because she loved it so much and taught it to so many children. We also sang some of the old camp songs and children's songs she loved, songs I had tried to sing for her that last moving-day: Fly Little Birdies; and Down Beside the Beautiful Sea. It's probably a good thing we didn't know the intercom was open to the mortuary office when we sang the one for which she'll always be famous, or infamous:
"In the Blue Ridge Mountains of Virginia
Stood a cow on the railroad track.
Such a lovely cow with eyes so fine,
But you can't expect a cow to read a railroad sign.
Along came a train on the track,
Hit the cow in the middle of the back,
Now the head's in the mountains of Virginia
And the tail's on the lonesome pine."
Good-bye Mom…know that you've left us smiling…5/3…
After the service, we hosted a "celebration supper" at our home. In the family tradition for any occasion of merit, we had a champagne toast. It was Jim who capped the evening.

"We always teased Granny about her fondness for champagne. At any party or event, I usually filled her glass first, as the oldest lady present, but by the time I'd get around the room to all the rest, Granny's glass would be empty, and she'd hold it up for more. So, Granny, have a toast with Pop tonight. Here's to you, turkey! We love you ... 5/3."

⚜

5/3 was Bessie's private code for the extra-special, Granny-sized love she had for her children and grandchildren.

I
think
I know
enough of hate
To say that for destruction
ice is also great
And would suffice.

Robert Frost
Fire and Ice

Six

Tip of the Iceberg

After Mom's memorial service, I looked forward to getting back to "normal." It literally had been years since things could be called normal around our household. But it wasn't many days before I realized things would never be normal again. The healing I thought had begun hovered elusively beyond my reach, mocking my good intentions. Although I wasn't sure where the next steps would lead, I realized that before I could experience closure, I needed to resolve the chaotic tangle of questions and emotions crowding my every waking moment. To be able to live with the awful fact of Mother's death, I knew I had to realize something positive from it. I determined to tell her story to anyone who would listen, so that no other frail old person would have to experience the terror and pain she had borne.

Telling Bessie's story in many different ways led to a variety of media opportunities, from the local newspaper, to a national magazine, to local and national radio and television appearances, to an interview with Mrs. Barbara Bush at the White House. To my great surprise, each presentation led to contacts with others who had experienced similar horrors. The resulting letters and phone calls confirmed that I was not alone. Gathered over several years from my work as an advocate, the material in this chapter has been taken out of chronological context, and is reported collectively here in order to substantiate the scope of elder abuse throughout the United States. These disgraceful instances of abuse and/or neglect (which constitutes abuse), have been extracted from case histories from files of my advocacy work. They represent examples from hundreds of cases from thirty-five states to date.

Hard statistics on elder abuse do not exist for several reasons. It is very difficult to prove. In recent years, more media attention has been given to elder abuse; however, the major emphasis has been on abuse in the home by a relative or hired caregiver. While there may be no witnesses to the abuse in the home, the fact of physical evidence and symptoms, as well as the presence and opportunity of the responsible person, often leads to prosecution.

The same kinds of abuse, with the same physical evidence and symptoms, in long-term care facilities can be nearly impossible to prove because so many caregivers are on the premises and so many plausible rationalizations are offered. If there is no eyewitness, there is seldom a fixing of blame. Even eyewitnesses are often ignored or discredited.

Many incidents of abuse go unreported. Fragile residents fear retribution. Even when the abuse is against another, a witness may fear for his/her own safety. There is lack of recognition of what abuse really is. Aides do not always recognize signs of abuse, or fear losing their jobs if they report. Even physicians do not always recognize abuse, incorrectly putting forward other reasons for physical evidence. Physical evidence is often passed off as natural bruising of aging skin or as resulting from a "natural" fall or from bumping into furniture or doors.

Families can be in denial, thinking that such things could not possibly happen, or not wanting to face the problems associated with confrontation. They fear retaliation if they "rock the boat." Many elders without family or friends to help them fear having to leave a familiar setting—even a hurtful one—if they complain. Many don't know how to register a complaint, or even that it is an option. The scarcity of affordable facilities makes finding a new one a formidable task.

Elder abuse seems to be an unmentionable problem until someone mentions it. Everywhere I told my story, people confirmed that they too had experienced problems with long-term care facilities. Consider that I am one person, founder of one advocacy nonprofit corporation. Consider the untold numbers of other family members and advocates and organizations across the nation. Consider the added factor of unreported abuse. When these incalculable numbers are considered, the picture of the iceberg is not unrealistic. There may never be a reliable method of verifying the magnitude of this problem, but it is very real, very frightening, and very widespread. Los Angeles City Councilman Joel Wachs has repeatedly termed it "a national disgrace." (Press conference, Los Angeles, CA, Sept. 5, 1991.)

Here is just a sampling of incidents of abuse and/or neglect from my files:

• Neglect of decubitis ulcers (bedsores) led to infection, sepsis, gangrene, and death.
• Always thirsty, requests ignored, water consistently out of reach, led to emergency hospitalization for dehydration.
• Obstructive mass in neck, noted on admission record; discrepancy in facility records, and physician's records; records re-dated; resident died, malignant mass.
• Unattended resident fell from bed, cried for help from floor, was found in respiratory distress; inadequate care was attributed to the death of another resident during that shift and to others needing assistance.
• Resident was left overnight in wheelchair in dark activities room, dressed only in gown, as "punishment" for calling out.
• Facility failed to provide necessary diabetic diet; improper insulin administration, insulin overdose; dehydration and death.
• Resident was yelled at, pinched, and later beaten by male aide who was bathing her.
• Residents walking halls with urine, feces, and vomit on their clothes.
• Forty-five-minute delay in answering call bells; treating wounds with non-sterile gloves.
• Resident observed naked beneath open dressing gown; later reported missing, picked up by two youths in a truck and deposited in neighboring town.
• Resident reported missing; not found in search of premises; later found lying at foot of little-used stairway.
• Immobile victim of multiple sclerosis burned by broken hot light

fixture that fell (damage of fixture had been previously reported by relative).

• Bowel blockage, treatment delayed, resident sent to hospital, bowel exploded, patient died.

• Diabetic resident was treated as stroke victim, given medication to raise blood sugar, went into coma, died.

• Resident left alone in chair in shower room fell, became paralyzed from neck down.

• Resident's kneecap shattered, resulting in amputation.

• Many reports of infected bedsores, some leading to amputations, some to death.

• Many reports of rough treatment, verbal abuse, indignities regarding personal privacy, rape.

• Many personal items stolen, gift packages undelivered.

• Many reports of neglected bedding changes: brown, dried urine stains, dried and embedded fecal matter.

• Many reports of pinching, rough handling, slapping, yelling, threats.

• Many reports of water withheld "because of increased bed changes necessary."

• Many reports of inappropriate food for condition of resident; food placed out of reach; trays picked up too soon; food jammed into mouth.

Elder abuse does happen. That it happens at all is a tragedy. That it happens frequently is a disgrace.

There seems to be no pattern regarding the victims. Residents whose families visit often are just as likely to be targets as those who have no family or advocate. But just imagine the plight of those who have no one to stand up for them.

Why does elder abuse happen?

- Lack of proper training and education of CNAs (Certified Nursing Assistants) who do most of the handling of residents, with specific emphasis on geriatric issues and indoctrination
- Too many residents to care for
- Low wages, little recognition or dignity afforded CNAs, engendering low self-esteem
- Language barrier: aides and/or residents sometimes speak limited English; different cultural standards; stress of job and of personal problems; working two shifts or two jobs; correct tone not demonstrated by administration of facility
- Corporate management is more concerned with the bottom line than with the human element

Finally, it must be mentioned that some residents themselves, through lack of understanding, personality changes, physical limitations, and lack of cooperation, may exhibit abusive behavior to their caregivers, resulting in abusive reactions. However, there is no excuse whatsoever for any professional caregiver, hired to give care, to retaliate. Nor is there any excuse for any facility to justify such actions.

These issues will be dealt with in detail in the following chapters.

*The Law,
wherein,
as in a magic mirror,
we see reflected
not only our own lives,
but the lives of all men
that have been!*

Oliver Wendell Holmes, Jr.
1885

SEVEN

THERE OUGHT
TO BE A LAW

"You *are* going to sue, aren't you?"
From the very first days after Mother's abuse, I don't know how many times people asked that question with its implied certainty. At the time it was all I could do to face each new day.

On the Monday following the abuse, after the traumatic assault of each new piece of information, I knew I needed to take the story to the top level of the nursing home management.

They needed to know what had happened in this facility. I found the name of the CEO on a piece of promotional literature in the nursing home lobby, and phoned his office to request an appointment. My call was not put through at the time, but I was told they would get back to me.

It took nearly seven months! And that was only after an open letter to every member of the board of directors of the corporation, outlining the attempts I had made, with copies of my correspondence and the unsatisfactory responses from the corporate office. I requested a meeting with the entire board, but was finally granted an appointment with the CEO, who also invited the president of long-term care, with whom I had met months before.

In the meantime, my frustration led to my making inquiries of an attorney. It was difficult to get across that I really wasn't interested in money, but in the facility's being held accountable for what had happened under its roof. The attorney gently addressed my naivete, explaining that the award of compensation is what proves the principle.

After looking at the pictures, he felt there was definitely basis for a suit, but that the time in the courts would likely be extensive, and the settlement not worth the investment.

After Mother died, I inquired of several law firms and was told by all that after a death in California there was, at that time, no recourse at all against the facility. This seemed the most incredible affront of all. The nursing home would not be held accountable for the merciless beatings that occurred while Mother was in their care! And I had no doubt that those beatings had contributed to her death six weeks later.

I was advised to take my material to the newspapers, but I was not yet ready to go that route. My emotions were too raw and I hadn't yet chosen a specific direction. The family needed time to heal and re-group. Our first granddaughter was born—the great-grandchild Mom never got to hold and rock. We took the cruise we'd been planning the night Mom passed away.

I needed to focus on something entirely new and different. Because of Mother's love of flowers, I had always loved designing and arranging, and had worked part time in a florist's shop, where I became good friends with the delightful owner. Pat gave me valuable training and encouragement as a floral designer, and later cultivated my dream of stepping out on my own. She helped me through the entire process of setting up my own custom design business. For over a year, the beauty of fresh flowers and silk surrounded me as I designed for weddings, receptions, showers, restaurants, and dinner parties, did interior design, and taught workshops. But it was all still there, just under the surface. I remained angry and frustrated. I learned during this time that the various investigations of Mother's case had been closed with no fixing of blame. After reading an article on nursing home investigations in *The Orange County Register*, I called reporter Jane Glenn Haas to inquire about it. She asked why I was interested. When I briefly shared Mother's story, she asked if I'd be willing to talk with her for publication. The focus was beginning to clear. I was ready now to take a stand, to do something. The subsequent article began a series of events that would change my life. The response, by mail and telephone, triggered the realization that other people were experiencing similar situations.

When I answered the phone one day, Marc Hankin introduced himself as an attorney with the Beverly Hills Bar Association. He had seen the newspaper article. He explained that he had long been interested in elder issues, and had recently drafted new legislation for the office of California Senator Mello, which, had it been in effect, would have made a difference in Mother's case.

He expected media coverage of the bill within a few weeks and wondered if I would consider appearing with him, as a family member who had experienced one of the very situations this bill would cover. I had promised myself I would tell Mother's story to anyone and everyone who would listen. Doors were opening. Now was the time.

"I would be delighted to," I told Marc Hankin.

There's going to be a law! I knew now where I could help make a difference.

※

It happened! On October 9, 1991, Governor Pete Wilson signed California Senate Bill 679, The Elder Abuse and Dependent Adult Civil Protection Act, which allows the families of abused elders—even after death—to bring suit. It also provides, upon a favorable verdict, for remuneration of attorney's fees and court costs by the perpetrator, and for possible determination by the court of a monetary award to the family.

There are laws, federal and state; there need to be others. The long-term care industry insists it is over-regulated, yet the lack of enforcement of laws and regulations, the loopholes, the waiving of fines, leave little incentive for compliance. And the abuse reports continue. In California alone, from 1988 to 1993, reported cases of abuse in institutional care climbed from 4,037 to 6,327, or a 57 percent increase (California Department of Aging, Office of the State Long-term Care Ombudsman report, January 1994, and Updated reports, Fiscal 1997, 1998). Complaints reported in 1997 and 1998 were 3470 and 4066 respectively, not an encouragingly significant change. This does not take into consideration the unreported cases. Again the iceberg lurks dangerously beneath the surface in the dark waters of inaction and non-accountability.

Because of a family trauma in his last year of law school, Marc Hankin has become a pioneering advocate in Elderlaw. He created Assembly Bill 2615, Spousal Protection Against High Cost of Long-term Care, which asserts the rights of Medi-Cal applicants to separate their community property without divorcing. Thanks to this bill, California law now dictates the automatic and equal division of a couple's assets on the day either one of them enters a nursing home. Only the nursing home resident's half must be spent down to qualify for Medi-Cal. Also, nursing homes have been required by law to inform patients and their families that their assets can be divided.

Even though my mother's abuse was investigated by the Ombudsman's office, the local Department of Health Services, Licensing and Certification, the local police authorities, the District Attorney, and the office of the Attorney General of the State of California Medi-Cal Fraud Division, no one was charged. Not even the facility was held accountable, because no hard proof of abuse could be attributed to the perpetrator. That was unacceptable to me, so I went to the state level Department of Health Services, Licensing and Certification in Sacramento (CA). As a result of their becoming involved, since July, 1992, Title 22 of the California Code of Regulations, Section 72527, has been amended to require long-term care facilities to ensure that a resident's right to be free from mental and physical abuse is not violated. In other words, facilities are not only responsible for care, but for the protection of the resident, as well. It took four long years to win this determination, which would in turn protect others.

This is a step in the right direction. But without a means of identification, alleged perpetrators have been known to leave one facility and move on to another. One such means of identification would be fingerprinting the employees of long-term care facilities. As of 1998,

California has legislated fingerprinting requirements. Standardization of fingerprinting requirements covering all staff of every type of care facility is needed throughout the United States. Why should we feel we've solved the problem by dismissing a suspected abuser, only to have him/her show up in the facility down the street?

Task Force committees, made up of knowledgeable participants, can perform a valuable service by studying existing legislation, evaluating and proposing new or amended legislation, and coordinating efforts between legislators to network information and advocacy. We would like to see coordination and cooperation between states through legislators, the Attorneys General, and even the governors.

There ought to be a law! There are laws, and there are more under consideration. But unless we are aware of and understand the laws, and unless they are enforced, laws can't guarantee the safety of our elders. As a starting point, we suggest the compilation of a printed guide outlining the laws currently in effect, in easily understood layman's terms. (Examples in California: *Nursing Home Companion: A User-Friendly Guide to Nursing Home Laws and Practices* and *How to Get Care From A Residential Care Facility*, prepared by Attorneys of Bet Tzedek Legal Services, Los Angeles.) This would be an invaluable resource for all caregivers. Please see Chapter 11, "Attention, Please, Families," and Chapter 14, "Attention, Please, Legislators and Government Officials" for further discussion of these issues.

No government action or agency, no advocacy or individual can ensure the elderly against abuse. Each family must take responsibility for its own loved ones.

All I know
is what I read
in the papers.

Will Rogers

EIGHT

A NATIONAL DISGRACE

꩜ We in the United States bear a national disgrace. Grandmas are beaten. Grandpas have amputations due to neglected bedsores. Aunts must undergo detoxification because they've been overmedicated in long-term care facilities. Moms are left alone to sit all night in wheelchairs.

What would convince you that these abuses occur all across our nation? Must it happen to someone you love?

I wasn't aware of it until it happened to my mom. Then I became convinced. I wanted it never to happen to anyone else. I had to do something. All I could do was tell her story.

I was given the opportunity when I was invited to appear on *Inside San Diego*, (San Diego, California). My first television experience! It was exciting and a little intimidating. I didn't know what to expect.

In making the arrangements on the telephone, the producer requested that I bring the abuse pictures to show on the program. That hit me in the stomach; I wasn't sure I could do it. I really didn't want people to see Mom like that. She was always so particular about how she looked. It was just second nature to me to protect her from that humiliation. Although I couldn't give them a positive answer, I assured the studio I would bring the pictures along, and make my final decision before the show.

We were to be at the studio very early in the morning so they could prepare the pictures for the camera in case I allowed them to be shown, and to prepare my face for the camera! Jim knew I was nervous. In his typical protective way he suggested we avoid the morning freeway traffic rush and drive down the coast the evening before. We checked into the motel and went out for a nice dinner. But I was still in turmoil when we got back to the motel. It was such a beautiful evening we decided to relax in the deserted Jacuzzi, where a young couple and their little son soon joined us. After greeting each other we drifted into conversation, which happens easily in California Jacuzzis: "Vacationing?" "Yes. You vacationing too?" "No, television show." "Oh, what about?"

I was careful of what I said because of the little boy, who looked about six years old. When he was distracted blowing bubbles, I quietly explained.

"I know something about that," the young father said. "My grandfather was hurt in a nursing home. It affected our whole family." I sensed the emotion under the words. As they left to take the boy to bed, the dad said he would be watching the show before they checked out in the morning.

My head was spinning again. I could feel the same outrage boiling up. Whenever I heard anyone else's story, I felt the same emotions and frustrations all over again.

As we finally walked back to the room, Jim asked quietly, "Have you decided to show the pictures yet?"

"Yes, I have." The visit with the family convinced me. In an uncanny way it was as if they arrived at just the right, quiet time to convince me. The indecision was over. I knew I had the pictures for a reason. Without their graphic proof, it's too easy for those unfamiliar with elder abuse to dismiss the awful reality. I could bear Mother's humiliation if it might protect another mother somewhere else. I slept soundly.

The next morning, I told Mother's story for the cameras. Before we left the studio there were phone calls. Once more, I knew I wasn't alone.

It wasn't long before Marc Hankin called again to tell me we had been scheduled for *The Home Show*, broadcast out of Los Angeles. Oh, wow! The Home Show! I've seen The Home Show! Everybody's seen The Home Show! Marc would be explaining what the law could do to protect elders, and specifically the new proposed legislation, California Senate Bill 679. Because my story was a "case in point" that so perfectly fit the legislation, I was to share from the family's viewpoint.

Preliminary calls from the producer informed me they'd send a driver so I wouldn't have to fight the rush-hour traffic from Orange County to Los Angeles. I was told not to bother with make-up or hair, because they would do that in the studio.

Not do hair or make-up? You've got to be kidding! It's like cleaning up the house before the cleaning lady comes. Of course I'd do hair and make-up!

I wasn't nervous about the story, but this was nationwide television. We had friends all across the country who would be watching. I had imaginary nightmares about showing up with mismatched shoes or something.

I was escorted to the room where I was to have my make-up and hair done. "They'll be with you in a moment, Mrs. Sandell," the escort said.

A distinguished-looking gentleman seated in the make-up chair turned upon hearing my name and said, "You must be Diane Sandell."

"And you must be Marc Hankin," I responded. "It's good to meet you."

There really is a "green room" where the guests wait before going on the show. It was fun to meet the others over sweet rolls with tea or coffee or juice, and to watch the earlier segments of the show on the monitor.

The interview went well and we were able to relax into the discussion, which went back and forth from my experience to Marc's proposed legislation. After it was over, the interviewer asked, "Have you two done this together before?" suggesting that familiarity accounted for the ease with which we presented our stories. It was fun to admit that we had just met for the first time.

A few weeks later, Marc called once again asking me to do a press conference at the Los Angeles City Hall, announcing the City Council's unanimous support for SB 679. I agreed with trepidation. My image of a press conference cast it with masses of aggressive news people pressuring for instant, spontaneous answers with defense and justification for those answers.

Councilman Joel Wachs had called the conference, and instead of just reading the motion of support, invited several people to share their stories, giving faces and details to the statistics.

Five times during the news conference, he referred to the problem as a national disgrace. It was the first time I had heard a government official use the term. I was filled with gratitude, respect, and new encouragement. We were given as much time as we wished to tell our stories. The media people were attentive and respectful. One told me how sorry he was that this had happened to my mother. Several media assistants came to me after the conference to ask personal questions about abuse. My image of a press conference was repainted that day.

Doris Winkler, host of the nationwide Senior Report, a program featuring issues of interest to senior citizens, asked to interview me after seeing the original article in the newspaper. She and her producer came to my home for the first interview. It was like visiting with friends. I served them tea. In ensuing months Doris did follow-up reports. I could always tell when one of the reports was aired, and in what part of the country, because my mailbox would overflow during those weeks, with mail from specific states where the show was broadcast.

I heard from and became friends with a personal advocate in Arkansas, and later was interviewed by Arkansas Public Service Television.

Several times I was a guest of Morgan Williams on her radio show, *The Big Picture*, on KBIG, in Los Angeles. Before the first interview, I asked whether we would review the questions she wanted to ask. She indicated she preferred the natural conversational style of unrehearsed dialog and said I could speak on anything I chose.

"And if you ask a question I feel I shouldn't discuss?" I asked hesitantly.

"You simply respond, 'I choose not to answer that question,'" she said with a smile.

As we went through the voice testing, Morgan told me about her mother having been in a hospital. She arranged to have a bed brought to the room so she could stay by her mother's side.

She said the long, noisy night in strange surroundings gave her an empathy with the fear that elderly people have when they are in unfamiliar situations.

Several years later, a freelance writer approached me about doing an article for *Family Circle* magazine. During the interview, all the feelings and emotions surfaced again. Though I had been doing advocacy work for several years, I had been so busy that I hadn't cried in a long time. It was a catharsis of sorts.

All these appearances brought heartbreaking letters. I answered every one with a letter or even a phone call. My phone bill skyrocketed. These people felt they had nowhere to turn. Because I'd gone through it, I felt I could at least point them in the right direction. It seemed something I could do in Mother's memory.

One man was told he'd have to take his wife out of the hospital in three days. She'd been neglected in several different nursing homes. He couldn't return her to any of those, and the others in the area were too distant for him to be able to visit. He was distraught. Because of the mail delivery, it was the last day by the time I received his letter. Hoping I could reach him, I picked up the phone and was relieved to be able to put him in touch with the local ombudsman. In a follow-up call I learned that they had been able to find a satisfactory place for his wife.

Then there was a letter from a woman, elderly and not well herself, whose mother, wearing only a light robe, had somehow wandered to the street in front of her nursing home. She was apparently picked up, driven to another town, and let out. The nursing home was dirty, rife with cockroaches, unwashed linens, unmade beds, vile smells, and neglected residents, but she had no choice. She could not bring her mother home.

What kind of answer can you give a person in such a situation? People had no idea where to go to get help. It wasn't that there were no agencies out there; people just didn't know where to go. I was convinced there was a big problem, one that was eating away at a whole generation of elders, as well as at their children who were their caregivers.

A national disgrace!

Are you convinced yet?
Would anything shock you into action?

⚬⚬⚬

The following is a copy of the motion made by Los Angeles City Councilman Joel Wachs in September 1991:

MOTION

Presented to the Los Angeles (CA) City Council
By Joel Wachs, Councilman, 2nd District

It is a sad fact of American life that elderly and dependent adults are vulnerable to physical, psychological or other abuses on the part of family members or other caregivers—those who are stronger than, or have other means of control over them. Incidents of abuse continue to be reported in many different forms, including physical isolation, physical attacks, verbal intimidation and harassment, starvation, unhealthful living conditions, and theft.

In 1990, the House Aging Committee estimated that more than 1.5 million elderly Americans each year may be victims of physical or mental abuse, most frequently by family members. Furthermore, the incidence of elder abuse nationwide was found to have increased by 50% since 1980.

Various federal and state legislative proposals have been made to reduce elder abuse, including SB 679 (Mello), which, among other things, would authorize the courts to award to the plaintiff attorney's fees and costs, including the cost of a conservator, where it is proven by clear and convincing evidence that a defendant is liable for physical abuse, neglect or fiduciary abuse of an elder or dependent adult and that the defendant has been guilty of recklessness, oppression, fraud or malice in the commission of abuse. The intent of this bill is to create additional incentives for attorneys to represent the victims of abuse, as well as to discourage acts of egregious abuse.

I Therefore Move that the City support SB 679 (Mello) and/or similar legislation which would authorize the award of attorney's fees and costs when it is proven by clear and convincing evidence that the defendant has been guilty of recklessness, oppression, fraud or malice in the commission of abuse.

Unanimously Approved September 4, 1991

Beware
of entrance to a
quarrel
but, being in,
Bear't that the opposed
may beware
of thee.

William Shakespeare
Hamlet

NINE

WE GO PUBLIC

꿹 Because of the response to the media appearances, from which I could not turn away, I found I was in a continual state of agitation. The desperation in these contacts demanded response. I found myself unable to shut it off.

Through my own experiences, I knew there were ways of getting attention, ways of getting action, ways of solving problems, ways of redirecting the hurt and frustration. I understood what it was like because I had been there. In spite of my empathetic indignation, I recognized that real healing was taking place for me as well, because I could see how to pass along to others what I had learned. Their concerns were today and needed attention today. My situation was past; nothing could change it. The door was closed for Bessie Jarvis, but was ajar on the future—a future dark with national shame unless we could turn the situation around.

An advocate with whom I had spoken gave me a great gift. "I believe you. I understand," were her first words to me, and, as I spoke with more and more people about their experiences, I was able to pass that gift along. "I believe you. I understand."

When we've experienced the abuse of an elder loved one, there are so many voices that try to dissuade us from the word abuse. By the industry and even by medical personnel, we have been told "No, no, he fell!" "Oh, but she's always bumping into things." "Their skin is so fragile, you know." "Don't you know how difficult he is to deal with?" From casual observers we hear, "Surely, you misunderstood." "I've never heard a bad report about that place." From some corners, we hear "Don't make so much of it." "Aren't you being obsessive about this?" But from those who have experienced the helpless heartbreak of going through the abuse of an elder loved one, their pain is proof enough. There is only acceptance and "I believe you. I understand." And when those are the first words of comfort I can offer another, it becomes a gift.

The frustration and helplessness expressed in the calls and mail convinced me of the need for an advocate for victims of abuse and their families. My advocacy became centered on helping the families. My guestroom quickly filled up with letters and files, news clippings, and supportive literature. The early correspondence was all hand-written; I couldn't type. Then friends took pity and typed for me. As the workload increased, I called Vicki, with whom I had done volunteer work in the past, to offer the position of "Volunteer Executive Secretary." She was often seen crawling around the guestroom on her hands and knees, searching out information from the files in boxes all around the room and closet. To mix metaphors, things were snowballing, and the fires of the hellish situations we were learning about didn't melt them away.

Friends and family urged me to make the advocacy official, and NOBLE (Network Outreach—Better Living for the Elderly) was born, and incorporated as a nonprofit grassroots corporation, complete with a board of directors that met, for some months, around my dining room table. Our stated purpose was to make people aware of the existence of and potential for abuse and neglect of the elderly in long-term care facilities, and to initiate action to improve elder care. Without the dedication and sacrifices of the board, NOBLE would not have been able to advocate for the elderly. The name NOBLE derived from ways of accomplishing the goals: networking, disseminating information, and outreach, resulting in better living for the elderly. Mother would have loved the name; Noble had also been my brother's middle name. We hoped that the searing flames of Bessie's pain and ours would light a torch of hope through educating others.

I began to tell our story to various groups, classes, service clubs, and philanthropic organizations. From the first, in public speaking and in private consultation, I related my background and history, and from that, my knowledge of the issues. Therefore my conclusions, advice, and recommendations were always prefaced with, "If it were my mother or father..."

When I presented our story at the First Presbyterian Church of Orange, they responded to the guestroom office situation by offering us an empty office, rent-free. In an indirect but very tangible way, they were ministering to the elderly, and I certainly felt I was part of their mission outreach. Beautiful new office furniture was donated through a local business. I created some silk floral arrangements and in we moved. The volunteer staff expanded a little through the generosity of friends and church members with their time. My time was also unpaid. I was a CEO with no salary, no car, no clothes, and no expense account, but I couldn't give up. We were just beginning to roll. Word was getting out that we were available. The number of people who found us in the telephone book surprised even me.

Networking came about through our involvement with other agencies and groups. I chaired California State Senator John Lewis's Task Force for the Elderly, and I strongly recommend such committees as an excellent way to obtain and to disseminate information and influence action. We were able to help families tell their stories in a wider forum as well as help the Senator and his colleagues better understand the reality of the problem. (See Chapter Fourteen, "Attention, Please, Legislators and Government Officials," and Appendix H for more details on task forces and cooperating with government representatives for improved elder care conditions.)

Because I knew the value of networking, I was willing to assume several additional roles in conjunction with the work of NOBLE. I sat on the boards of directors of the Orange County Council on Aging—Ombudsman, and of FATE (Foundation Aiding the Elderly) in Sacramento, California. I served on two other committees: the Long-term Care Consumer Advocates of the State Licensing and

Certification Committee, Sacramento, California; and the Alzheimer's Association Public Policy Committee of Orange County. In each of these groups the reciprocal benefits of exchange of information, suggestions, and resources resulted in a growing pool of help for elders and their families.

From these and other contacts, NOBLE created and maintained a library of resources: brochures, pamphlets, books, articles, catalogs, clippings, and videos, as well as announcements and schedules of various classes, seminars, and workshops to which we often sent representatives. We also obtained information regarding resources, services, and advocacies in other states, from which clients could get help, and from which I could obtain resources for callers from other states.

We visited long-term care facilities throughout the area to keep aware of conditions. We made it a policy never to recommend facilities; that had to be a family's decision. But we were available to accompany families when they were trying to resolve problems in facilities or with agencies such as Licensing. It was from just such instances that we created the Five-Point Plan for evaluating elder care and resolving problems (discussed in Chapter Fifteen and Appendix F).

Despite the generous provision of office space, funding for operation was always difficult. There was never a cost to clients or families requesting help, and in the early days I never asked a fee for speaking to groups. I just wanted the information out there. Most of our funds were donated by friends and relatives, organizations to which I had spoken, and occasionally by families whom we had helped. Recognition awards in 1992 and 1993 from the Soroptimist International of Orange, and a Disneyland Community Service Award in 1994, came as pleasant surprise boosts to the budget, but regular funding was extremely difficult to find. As widespread as the problem is, and as vital as the work of solving it is, our society pretends the problem doesn't exist. Therefore we don't fund to solve the problem.

Because of lack of funding, NOBLE had to close its doors in 1995. It was one of the hardest things we have ever had to do. The phones were still ringing even after the official closing of the doors, right up till we pulled the last plug. One more call. One more request. One more plea. Another advocate asked, "But where will we send the families?"

NOBLE was a gift to me. It provided the means to an end: closure of Mother's "chapter."

NOBLE was her gift to others. It provided families with the means to address and solve their own problems and, ultimately, find closure.

NOBLE still exists in spirit. Everywhere I go I still meet people who are experiencing problems and don't know where to turn. I still tell the story, still try to help. This book carries forward the purposes and goals of NOBLE—to advocate "Better Living for the Elderly."

Because of opportunities and circumstances that have arisen in the years since NOBLE closed, plans are underway to re-open NOBLE as an advocacy resource. You may access information about NOBLE at www.NOBLEusa.org

For
Memory
has painted
this perfect day
With colors that never fade,
And we find at the end
of a perfect day
The soul of a
friend
we've made.

Carrie Jacobs Bond
A Perfect Day

TEN

MEETING MILLIE AND MRS. BUSH

◄¹ We were having a quiet morning. It was too hot outside to consider going out. The air conditioning unit was noisily but
efficiently making the dining room pleasant. My sister Betty Lane,
visiting from Pennsylvania, had just refilled our teacups as I pulled
muffins from the toaster oven.

"Maybe we'll head to the beach for dinner tonight," I offered as we
buttered hot muffins. "It will surely be cooler there."

The phone jangled, breaking into our companionable lethargy.

"Hello?"

"Mrs. Diane Sandell?"

"Yes," I responded, wiping crumbs from my mouth.

"This is Randa Mendenhall calling from Mrs. Barbara Bush's office at the White House."

※

In NOBLE's quest to make the public aware of the dangers threat-
ening our nation's senior population, I had appeared on several
television and radio shows, and was receiving mail from all over the
United States with chilling confirmation that my experience was
not an isolated event. The potential for elder abuse touches virtually every family in the nation and the world. Barring catastrophic
illness or accidental death, we will all face the challenges of growing
old. Until people realize and accept the fact that this is a universal
problem that affects them personally, they tend to dismiss the subject altogether. I hoped to enlist a highly visible, credible spokesperson

who, by his/her involvement and valid indignation, would help spread the message. Informed awareness will go far in helping to curb and solve this national disgrace.

I wrote to every high-profile name I could think of: government officials, local, state and nationwide, whose attention and sponsoring legislation could make a difference; media personalities who present social issues in formats seen by millions; movie and television actors who had starred in stories about issues facing the elderly; and the First Lady of our land, Mrs. Barbara Bush. After my initial correspondence with Mrs. Bush's office, I had been sending updates of my work for her information and files.

⸛

The air conditioner murmured into the silence as, wide-eyed, I mouthed the words "White House!" to my sister.

I'm not sure what amenities we spoke. I was too incredulous to take it all in, but we spoke for a number of minutes. Ms. Mendenhall acknowledged and thanked me for all the materials I had previously sent, assured me of Mrs. Bush's interest and appreciation, and invited me to continue submitting materials and information on elder abuse.

Throughout the following months, whenever I sent materials for their files, I frequently had calls from Ms. Mendenhall on Mrs. Bush's behalf. It became a family joke between the kids as they'd call me to the phone: "It's the White House again, Mom." Seriously, I had developed a great rapport with Ms. Mendenhall, and felt that in her I had found a caring friend and a valuable advocate.

In the spring of 1992, *Family Circle* magazine published a bit of our story in their feature column, "Women Who Make A Difference." Although I was disappointed that the coverage had to be limited to fit the feature format, it was exciting to see references to our advocacy in print. By this time I felt a true friendship with Randa Mendenhall, and immediately called to blurt out that the magazine was on the stands. I offered to fax a copy of the article, but imagine my delight when she said, "Don't! I'll go out on my lunch hour and get a copy."

Several days later, Randa called again. After sending the magazine article through to Mrs. Bush's desk, she'd had a note from Mrs. Bush inquiring if it might be advisable to set up a meeting with me on some future trip to California. With my heart in my mouth, I responded that I planned to be on the East Coast in June, and would be delighted to schedule a meeting there at her convenience.

What a thrilling possibility to cap an already exciting trip. In June 1992, my sister, Betty Lane, would be retiring from her position as a kindergarten teacher in Everett, Pennsylvania. Friends and associates planned a surprise honorary dinner to which I was invited, all the way from California. Since Betty Lane and I talked frequently by phone, it was no small task keeping the dinner a surprise, and now I had this new secret to keep.

Finally the week of her retirement came. All the "cover stories" were in place and I was on the way. Jim was not planning to travel with me, but I couldn't risk her calling and reaching him if I were away from the house. I had told her that Jim and I were getting away for a little break in our routine and wouldn't be home, but in an emergency the kids would know how to reach us. One of Betty Lane's friends picked me up at the airport and delivered me to a local motel where I "hid out." I couldn't even risk being seen in town, where I knew many of her friends. The next evening I slipped into the dining room and melted into the crowd of well wishers awaiting her arrival. Because of the surprise of the party and of seeing so many gathered to greet her, it took her awhile to realize I was actually in the crowd.

Later that evening, as we sipped tea in her living room and looked over the many cards, flowers, and gifts, we reminisced about the many times we'd had just such bedtime chats after momentous occasions in our lives.

"Betty Lane," I said, kicking off my shoes and stretching.

"Um?" she said contentedly.

"You remember how you always used to take me everywhere with you when we were kids?"

"Yes, all my friends used to tease me about draggin' the kid along."
"Well, it's payback time." I savored the moment. "The kid's going
to drag you somewhere next week."

"Oh?"

"How would you like to meet Barbara Bush?"

"You're really going!" She had known of my correspondence.

"Nothing's promised, but it's a growing possibility."

We didn't get much sleep that night.

The following week, though I had appointments with several advocates in Washington, I had not yet contacted Randa nor heard from
her. Betty Lane and I and her friend, Dorothy, who was our hostess,
were lunching at Union Station when Dorothy called her home to
speak with her husband. She hurried back to the table with the message that the White House had called trying to locate me. I was up
like a shot, found a phone and dialed Randa's number, which I now
knew by heart. When she answered, she got right to the point.

"We've been trying to reach you. Mrs. Bush had wanted to meet
with you today, but ..."

"Does that mean it's not going to happen?" I asked, with sinking heart.

"Actually, no. She offered an alternate time, and could meet with
you at noon tomorrow, if you are ..."

"I'm free!" Actually, I had an appointment I'd have to break, but I
rather felt they'd understand.

"Guess what!" I said as I returned to the table. "We're going to the
White House tomorrow!"

We called to make appointments to have our hair done first thing
the next morning, and spent the rest of the afternoon like schoolgirls
discussing our wardrobe options. That evening, I received telephone
calls from various aides explaining what to expect, procedures, and
security checks. Although I had known I'd be allowed to bring my
sister who had come to Washington with me, it was a generous bonus
that I could invite Dorothy, who would be driving for us. A tiny dark
cloud hovered over the statement that there were, of course, no ab-
solute guarantees, for Mrs. Bush could be called away at any time.

I spent a restless, wakeful night. Would we really get to see her? Would my hair be all right? Would I look okay? Would we get there on time? Would there be a lot of traffic? How much time would I have with Mrs. Bush? Would we really get to see her?

It suddenly dawned on me that I didn't know how much time had been allotted for our visit. I knew this would be my only chance to share my concerns face to face and although I was experienced in giving two-hour seminars, I realized I would be fortunate to have only five or ten minutes with the First Lady. The rest of the night, between fitful naps, I refined my story to the most vital essence possible.

The day dawned hot and sticky as only Washington can be. We received an early call confirming the noon appointment with Mrs. Bush. Betty Lane and I trooped to the beauty salon for fresh hairdos. We were giddy and giggly. We were going to meet the First Lady!

At the first gate it was exhilarating to tell the uniformed guard we had an appointment with Mrs. Bush. After checking his appointment list and Dorothy's driver's license, he passed us through to the second gate, where we were met by a guard with a formidable-looking German shepherd. The dog efficiently inspected the car and the trunk.

"I hope headache prescription with codeine doesn't offend him," I whispered to Betty Lane, referring to my emergency traveling bag in the trunk. It didn't, and we were passed through to where we should park, and walked to the third gate. There a guard checked all our identification, and commented to Betty Lane that he came from a Pennsylvania town near hers.

Then it was through the metal detectors. Betty Lane and Dorothy stepped right through. Guess what! Diane set off all the alarms! Red-faced, I removed my heavy metal bracelet and earrings while a guard looked through my briefcase. Feeling a bit naked, I stepped through the now-silent detector and retrieved my traitorous jewelry.

We were getting closer! Just inside the portico, a gentleman rose from behind a mahogany desk and ushered us into a waiting room. The first things I noticed were the beautiful fresh flowers. A woman stepped through the door and came to me, saying, "I'm Randa."

Although we'd never seen each other before, we instinctively hugged. We were escorted upstairs to an office where we met other volunteers and staff.

"May I take pictures?" Betty Lane asked Randa, indicating her camera.

"Oh, Mrs. Bush has arranged for the White House photographer to take pictures."

We were then taken into the China Room, where the china from various administrations is displayed. With a thrill, I recognized the Eisenhower china from pictures I'd seen.

A member of Mrs. Bush's staff entered and went through the protocol, explaining that Randa would introduce us to the First Lady. We'll get five minutes at most, I thought, but I was still wondering if it would really happen. We were escorted to the Diplomatic Reception Room, where heads of state are received, I thought giddily.

Everything became silent. I turned to see Millie padding through the door, making the rounds, allowing each of us in turn to pet her. We're on! As we were all smiling and making over Millie, Mrs. Bush appeared in the doorway, followed by a Secret Service agent who quickly glanced around the room. We must be okay, I thought as he stepped back into the hallway, discreetly near but apart from us. The photographer materialized from somewhere and was already snapping pictures as Randa presented us to Mrs. Bush. She was indeed the First Lady of the land and of the White House, but the "lady of the house" as well. I felt like a friend, a guest in her home. I felt I could have invited her to tea in my own home.

"It is a pleasure to meet you, Mrs. Bush," I said. "Actually this is my second visit to the White House. I had the opportunity to meet Mrs. Eisenhower when my school class visited Washington. We met her in the State Dining Room and presented her with roses...oops," I gasped. "I should have brought flowers!"

"Oh, I have lots of flowers," Mrs. Bush laughed, trying to make me feel comfortable after what I considered a faux pas.

"Mrs. Bush," I started again, not wanting to impose upon her generosity, "I believe you know why I am here, and what happened to my mother."

"Yes, I've seen the pictures."

I was impressed that this was not just a courtesy visit. She'd done her homework. I had previously sent pictures of Mother's abuse, as well as other information on abuse of the elderly.

Remembering my homework of the long night before, I briefly explained that Mother's case was definitely not an isolated incident; that determination to prevent any other family from going through what we'd gone through led to the founding of NOBLE; and a bit about NOBLE's work and goals. I expressed the desire that we make everyone aware of the problems and work together for a solution for the elderly of our nation.

"Mrs. Bush," I said, sensing that our time might be drawing to a close, "I would like to present you with a certificate of appreciation from NOBLE to thank you for your caring and concern for our work."

"Thank you," she replied quietly, "but you really should be giving this to Randa."

"No," I whispered. "I have one to present to her in a few minutes." Then aloud, "Mrs. Bush, I also have brought a packet of NOBLE's materials to share with you."

"Thank you," she said. "I will share them with the President."

I was thrilled! She could not have offered me a greater gift.

Mrs. Bush then graciously turned and visited personally with Betty Lane and Dorothy for a few moments before she said good-bye. With amazement I realized she had given us nearly thirty minutes of her time.

Randa concluded our visit with a private tour of the White House, during which we especially enjoyed seeing the calligraphy office, where all the social invitations are lettered by hand. As we descended a staircase, through the frame of a window on the landing we observed a peaceful, serendipitous scene. In a silent panorama, Millie frolicked across the White House lawn as Mrs. Bush strolled behind, followed closely by her ever-present Secret Service agent.

I caught my breath. A perfect end to a perfect day.

DIANE SANDELL WITH MRS. BARBARA BUSH
Photo by Carol Powers/White House Photographer

Epilogue

"Bessie's Legacy"

Dear Mom,

I don't know where to begin! It's been such an exciting week! I actually got to meet Mrs. Bush at the White House. Oh, Mom, I wish you could have been there. But you are the reason I got to go, Mom, and I really think you were there with "your girls."

The funniest thing happened as we came out of the White House. As soon as we came through the gates, we all headed for telephones. We looked like the press corps trying to scoop the latest headline.

I called Jim at work, Mom, and his secretary said he was in a meeting. I told her I really needed to have her call him to the phone for just a moment. When he came on the line I think I must have babbled on and on trying to tell him all the details. Finally, he just said quietly, "That's really great, Honey. I can tell it was a real thrill for you. Could we discuss this further tonight? I really have to get back to my meeting."

NOBLE was created for you, Mom. I know it was too late to save you from hurt and fear, and that will always be a source of great sadness for me. But I have to move on from that point and turn it into something good for someone else. You were always doing things for others in your sweet gentle way. By doing our best to make people aware of the problems, and offer some helpful advice, maybe we can help save other dear souls from going through your pain. That could be a great legacy in your memory. Perhaps, one day, we can truly offer "Better Living for the Elderly." I hope we can do that, Mom, with all my heart.

I love you, Mom, 5/3, still and always, XXXOOO, Your Di

The
difficulty
in life
is
the
choice.

George Moore

Eleven

Attention, Please, Families

⊰ No government action or agency, no advocacy foundation or individual can ensure the elderly against abuse. There are laws, there are agencies, there are advocacy groups and still abuse happens. It is up to each individual to accept responsibility for doing whatever he or she can, in whatever capacity, to end the national disgrace of elder abuse.

And that means you, and you, and you.

Each one of us could face the prospect of caring for another or needing care ourselves at some time in our lives. Start where you are. Each family must take responsibility for ensuring the best possible care for its elder loved one, whether in the elder's own home, the family's home, or in a long-term care facility. For some this may be an easily accepted labor of love. For others, traumatic family history may cause you to want to reject this duty. Regardless of your personal feelings, it is a responsibility.

What does this responsibility mean?

It means understanding the needs of the elder. Chapter Fifteen, "Evaluating Your Elder's Care," offers suggestions to help assess your elder's situation and needs, to determine some of the details of everyday living, to find helpful resources, and to provide quality care at any stage of need.

It means understanding the changes and tensions associated with caregiving. Things are different. Relationships are different. Chapter Sixteen, "Coping With the Dirty Dozen," provides suggestions for dealing with the most common tensions of caregiving.

It means a cooperative effort between the caregiver and the

immediate family for the most satisfactory possible arrangements for living with the added responsibilities, concerns, demands, and, yes, rewards of contributing to the success of the loved one's elder years.

In Chapters Twelve, Thirteen, and Fourteen, we challenge medical personnel, long-term care facility personnel, and government officials, to consider and accept their responsibilities and to initiate changes in their fields of expertise. But because the primary responsibility must lie with the family, we challenge families to become informed, educated and involved. We urge you to partner with all these professionals, and thereby take responsibility for the overall care and protection of the elder.

PARTNERING WITH MEDICAL PROFESSIONALS

The primary caregiver within the family should take the initiative in meeting and getting to know mom's physician, who is a real person with a real life apart from the antiseptic atmosphere of the examining room. Most physicians are very approachable; from the earliest stages of care, they encourage contact with other family members. As one concerned physician said, "It's easier and less stressful for all to establish links before crises arise."

If you are taking mom to the physician's office, it works well for the caregiver to go into the examining room with mom, share needed information, and hear specific directions concerning care. Then allow mom some private time with the physician to discuss anything she might prefer to keep confidential.

If dad is in a long-term care facility, it is more difficult to meet with the doctor; however, you could request a specific appointment at his convenience when he is scheduled to visit the facility. As the overseeing caregiver, mediate between dad and the physician, facilitating the applicable suggestions in Chapter Twelve. Help it happen.

Don't judge mom's compatibility with the doctor too quickly. The first few visits may be awkward—give it time. Keep open, cooperative communication with the doctor. After a number of visits, if mom's discomfort continues, it may be appropriate to request another physician. Don't be intimidated. It is in everyone's best interest that the loved one be comfortable with his/her physician of record. If mom has a history of inability to accept and cooperate with her physician, you may have to use your judgment in determining what is best for her, and stand by your decision.

PARTNERING WITH LONG-TERM CARE FACILITIES

Chapter Fifteen will help you evaluate your elder's need for more care. If the indications are that a skilled long-term care facility is the best choice for care, Appendix D will help you make an informed decision.

When you place a family member in a facility, OBRA (Omnibus Budget Reconciliation Act of 1987, a federal regulation containing major nursing home reforms, primarily in the area of residents' rights) requires the facility to schedule an assessment meeting and a care-plan meeting with the family and staff members overseeing the resident's care. In order to be assured that all your questions and concerns are addressed, be prepared with your own list of topics and questions. As with the medical personnel, it is vital to indicate not only your willingness, but also your intent and requirement to "be there" whenever there is need.

On the day of admission, take a picture of mom (or dad) with the front page of the daily newspaper, showing the date, facing the camera. Why? It gives you a dated record to show how mom looks on the day of admission. (If the date is not discernible in the original print, the photo can later be enlarged if necessary.) Some video cameras record the date automatically. If she is able to walk, show her walking into the building. This gives you a visual dated record that we hope will be only a pleasant picture for your family album. But it is also a valuable tool to use as a guide to monitor the progressive state of your loved one's condition. In the event of any question concerning mistreatment or abuse, there will be a recorded "before" picture for comparison with later conditions.

Every time you visit, have a camera and a dated portion of the newspaper with you. If you notice any bruise marks, even if there is an apparent logical explanation, take a picture. For dad's peace of mind, try to do it naturally, without comment, taking the picture of dad, not just of his bruises. Keep these pictures on file to review further if there should be any major incident later.

Purchase a notebook and, from the first day of admission, start a journal with a dated entry made every visit, like a diary. This can "entertain" your elder as you visit, interviewing him about his activities, any comments on television shows he's watched or magazines or books he's read, friends he's made among the other residents or staff, and any concerns he expresses. Note anything he might request you to bring on a future visit, any questions, and any complaints, minor or major. Note dad's demeanor and attitude, his physical appearance and grooming, appetite, and general outlook. Listen to what dad tells you. If he says something you find hard to believe, accept it to the extent of checking it out. Don't just automatically dismiss it. Like the photographs, the journal will give you a running account, progressively, by which to monitor dad's physical and mental states. It will also give you a tool by which to evaluate any unusual occurrences, any patterns.

Establish rapport with the staff. Be cooperative and helpful. Give credit where credit is due. If there are minor things you can assist with, do so, but be definite about what you need and expect. For example, "I noticed Mom's water pitcher was empty, so I filled it. She really needs to have it closer to her so she can reach it. Her medications make her extremely thirsty."

Your cooperation shows you aren't always demanding; however, your main concern is the care of your loved one. If you disagree with something the facility is doing, learn the lines of authority so you can speak with the right person to address your needs. If it has to do with actual health care, speak to the floor nurse in charge, usually a Registered Nurse (RN) or a Licensed Vocational Nurse (LVN). If your request is not addressed, it may be necessary to go to the director of nursing or the physician. If it has to do with non-medical or general housing care, go to the appropriate department: dietitian, social services, housekeeping, activities, laundry, etc.

Again, if it is not resolved, you may need to speak with the administrator. Because of the changing shifts, it is not usually productive to make requests of the aides. It will ease your concerns and frustrations to speak to the one with the authority to initiate action or change.

By following these recommendations, you are doing your job as the family caregiver. You are visiting as often as possible, you are noting your observations in writing, and you are acting on your observations.

If you are ever confronted with major or suspicious bruising, take action at once. Ask mom how it happened. Ask the director of nursing what medical treatment has been done or is needed. Ask whether the incident has been reported to the doctor and to the ombudsman. Ask whether a report has been made to the Licensing and Certification Department, or even to the police. Ask if it was entered on the medical records and ask to see the records, as is your right if you hold a Durable Power of Attorney for Health Care. (See Chapter Fifteen, Paragraph A.3 and Appendix C for further discussion of this invaluable tool.) You also have the right to see the patient's medical records with mom's permission if she is able to give it. Take close-up pictures from several angles (using today's dated newspaper). It is recommended that you, as the overseeing caregiver, call the ombudsman on your own, even if the facility has already done so. This puts you on record, reporting your concerns as the family representative.

If the trauma is obviously a major one, and the facility has not done so, call the police at once. The family must not be susceptible to the fear factor—fear of mistaken judgment, fear of retaliation. Only by reporting such incidents will we eventually gain control over them. If you don't do something about your own experience, it will be repeated with another family, and another, and perhaps even yours again. Each family must take responsibility for its own loved one, but in the reporting factor, the dissemination of information and the resulting disciplinary action against the perpetrators will help prevent further abuses.

Partnering with Legislators
and Government Officials

If you experience an incident of abuse, consider notifying your government representatives by mail or by telephone. Explain that you realize they are not law enforcement, but that you simply want them to be aware of the types of things that are going on in violation of the regulations governing long-term care facilities. If you choose to report in person and are granted an appointment, respect the legislator's time and go prepared.

Explain that you want them to be aware of situations in long-term care facilities in their district.

Briefly explain the circumstances of the abuse.

Take your dated "before and after" pictures and your journal to show that you have documented your loved one's residence at the facility.

Explain what the facility has or has not done to resolve this situation.

Explain that you will keep the legislator informed of the progress of the situation.

Ask if the legislator has established a task force for elder issues.

In Chapter Fourteen, "Attention, Please, Legislators and Government Officials," we urge government representatives to inform themselves on this vital issue of elder abuse and to take responsibility in their field to address the problem. We have recommended and outlined the establishment of task forces, which are committees on any designated subject for the purpose of keeping legislators informed on various issues, and providing a vehicle for necessary change.

Any legislator can sponsor a task force for elder issues, and we ask all legislators to consider establishing such committees in their areas for the purpose of becoming informed, networking information, and creating united, coordinated legislative action to correct the problems of elder abuse.

Chairing such a task force is something you or another member of your family might consider offering to do for your legislator. When I met with California Assemblyman John Lewis the day before he was elected state senator, I told him about the senior citizen task force previously sponsored by his predecessor. After he was elected, Mr. Lewis chose to sponsor, and asked me to chair his Task Force for the Elderly. (The composition of Mr. Lewis' task force is outlined in Appendix H, and may be used as an example if your legislator does not yet sponsor one.)

CLOSURE AFTER ABUSE

Once you have experienced an incident of abuse in a long-term care facility, after you have notified the ombudsman and/or the police as well as a local advocacy group, there will be a time of waiting while those agencies make their investigations. In California, the facility must notify the Department of Health Services, Licensing and Certification. They must also notify the ombudsman or the local police department. In California and in other states, the ombudsman can inform you of the required reporting procedures for your state, and advise you how to keep informed of the status of the investigation.

The result could be a finding anywhere in a broad range, from no accountability to full accountability with resulting disciplinary action. If the finding is acceptable to you, so be it. However, if you do not agree with the finding, you may take further action as described in the written notification from the Licensing and Certification Department. In California you may request a hearing to cite your disagreement with the finding and to appeal the decision. Be prepared to take all your documentation, photos, journal, and any new facts you may be aware of. Request that Licensing re-open and re-investigate the incident. (See Appendix G for assistance in preparing for this meeting.) If the new finding is still unacceptable, you have the recourse of requesting an investigation by the state level office overseeing this department. Of course, at any time in the process you have the option of seeking legal advice and filing civil action against a facility or an individual.

You and your family must decide upon a goal that will provide closure for you. You really cannot put this behind you and move on until you define what will end it for you, personally. Perhaps you will consider one of the investigative findings appropriate and acceptable. However, if that is not the case, you need to determine that you have done everything that you yourself can do. For some, this means active advocacy work. For some, it means support groups. For some, it means telling your story to the media. For some, it means getting active politically. For some, it means volunteering. For some, it can be as simple as handholding for another family suffering this situation.

Even when you have accepted that you have done everything possible and are able to close the doors on this chapter, you will still experience moments of remembrance. Some may be bittersweet and destructive. You have to learn to live with those moments, and choose to close the door again.

You do what you can do, and what you need to do, and then you decide when you have closure.

Attention, please, families.

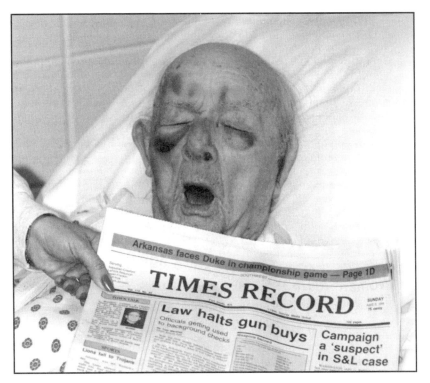

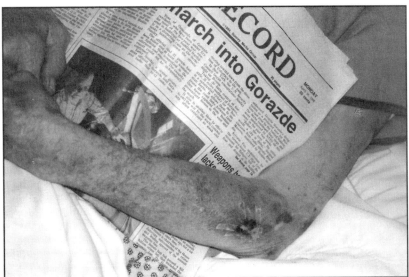

NEWSPAPER DOCUMENTS THE DATE OF ABUSE

95

I swear
that I will carry out,
according to my ability and judgment,
this oath...I will use treatment to help the sick
according to my ability and judgment,
but never with a view to injury and wrongdoing.
I will keep pure and holy both my life and my art.
In whatsoever houses I enter, I will enter to help the sick,
and I will abstain from all intentional wrongdoing and harm.
Now if I carry out this oath, and break it not,
may I gain forever reputation among all men
for my life and for my art;
but if I transgress it and
forswear myself,
may the opposite
befall me.

The Physician's Oath
Hippocrates
460–377 B.C.

TWELVE

ATTENTION, PLEASE, PHYSICIANS
AND MEDICAL PERSONNEL

Many of us grew up with a "God fixation" about our physicians and medical personnel. Doctors' offices, hospitals, and testing labs were places where hushed voices, antiseptic odors and crisply starched uniforms inspired respectful awe tinged with fear. We crowned our medical heroes with halos of infallibility, never presuming to question or challenge any decision, recommendation, or treatment.

The age of easy lawsuits has changed all that. On the positive side, we have protection and recourse for mistaken or truly inadequate treatment. On the negative side, however, frivolous lawsuits have inordinately driven up the cost of maintaining insurance protection, further raising costs of treatment and further elevating frustration on both sides of the examination room. We place our heroes on pedestals, then contribute to nudging them off.

Humanizing our medical professionals does have advantages. To assure the best overall health care program for any patient (in the case of the focus of this book, the care of our elders), the medical professional, the elder and his/her family, and the personnel of long-term care facilities need to learn to work cooperatively.

Many of the suggestions that follow in this chapter are simply common sense and good human relations in any situation, but are sometimes overlooked in our hurried, harried, fast-paced lifestyle. We respectfully ask that the physicians and other medical personnel who read these words accept them in the spirit in which they are offered.

97

We also ask family members and other non-medical personnel to consider these suggestions reciprocally. Both the positive and the negative examples are taken from the many cases I have personally worked with. No finger pointing is intended; there is only the hope for better relations all around, win-win situations and results.

All Medical Personnel, Please:

Introduce yourself distinctly, by title, on your first contact. If the patient's mental awareness necessitates it, repeat on successive visits.

As a matter of respect, use patients' last names and titles (Mr., Mrs., Miss, Dr., Rev., etc.). Don't use first names unless specifically requested to, or familiar non-names (Dear, Honey), which can be demeaning. These elders deserve the dignity too frequently stripped from them when they become dependent upon assisted living arrangements. They have contributed to society as parents, teachers, scientists, doctors, attorneys, clergy, musicians, writers, artists, businessmen and women, lawmakers, merchants, and technicians.

See your patients as real human beings, and not as case files. Take the time to learn about their personal histories as well as their medical histories.

Make yourself aware of the circumstances surrounding the elders in your care, whether you attend them in their own or a caregiver's home, in an office or lab setting, in a long-term care facility or in the hospital.

Consider that, like children, many of these elders are frightened because they are no longer in control. They don't like or understand the changes in their lives. Win their trust and respect by treating them with dignity and respect. If you are considerate, and the patient is cognizant of what is going on, they'll respond in kind. If you are abrupt and impersonal, a negative reaction is likely. In my mother's case, facility personnel referred to her several times as "combative," as if that excused the fact that someone beat her twice in one night while she was restrained in a posey, unable to strike out or protect herself. As a matter of record, the psychiatrist who had earlier been called in to examine her cited her hospitable graciousness throughout the interview, and her expressed regret that she couldn't offer him a cup of tea. She was responding in kind to the manner in which he treated her.

By reason of your objectivity you may be able to help elders and their families better understand a situation in a care facility, and help facility personnel better understand the care of residents. Better understanding on all sides results in more satisfactory care and more satisfied residents and families.

While some personal family physicians visit facility residents, if your services are referred through the facility, you need to be the resident's physician, not the facility's physician. By virtue of your Hippocratic oath, your first concern must be for your patient.

Physicians need to be direct with the facility; if the facility isn't doing the job, you have the power and the responsibility to exert influence. The physician should be "the boss" of the resident's care. Treatment should be for the good of the resident, not the convenience of the facility.

Physicians need to be direct with the family of the resident. If the family isn't doing its job in support of its elder, you have the influence to make recommendations that might result in a better atmosphere. Whenever possible, maintain open communication with the family.

In the case of a long-term care facility resident who does not have any family, you may be the only outside influence in that person's life. Because of the ages of this particular generation of residents, and their ingrained regard for your profession, you have the power to greatly enhance their lives with encouraging, understanding support. Take the time to acquaint yourself with residents as much as they are able to respond. Don't just take cold data from a case file.

There is an inside joke about doctors being the worst patients. Consider what it might be like if you were in the resident's bed. We ask caregivers to imagine infirmities like weakened eyesight and hearing, arthritic joints, immobility, painful medical conditions, and loss of dignity. We also ask medical personnel to take the time to consider these limitations. Just as we drill medical teams for emergency situations, it might be worth a graphic role-playing exercise in a training seminar to demonstrate these limitations, using medical personnel as the infirm elders.

If more than one physician treats a resident, check past records, consider the effects, interactions, and reactions of multiple medications and the possible adverse results. There have been many cases of drug use for behavior control and restraint, resulting in inactive, incoherent, non-functioning patients. In some fortunate cases, discontinuing excessive medication has resulted in the resident reverting to normal functioning behavior.

Regarding physical abuse, physicians, remember you are mandated reporters. Don't be hasty to dismiss bruising as natural for older skin, the results of bumps and falls. The facility physician dismissed the bruising on the top of my mother's head as possibly resulting from a fall; the handprint on her face was rationalized as having possibly been caused when someone picked her up! This could only have happened had she fallen directly onto the top of her head and been picked up by her face! Learn the signs of covert abuse. Consider the humanity of the resident and let your righteous indignation determine your advocacy. Look for repeat bruising. Ask members of the staff, not just the management, what the climate is in the facilities you visit. Many nurses and aides have reported being afraid to blow the whistle for fear of losing their jobs; others who reported abuse situations have lost their jobs. Be an advocate for those who are trying to do their jobs well and compassionately.

If the physician is doing the job properly, he or she will already be doing these things. We do not intend to insult your intelligence with these commonsensical suggestions. However, there are far too many instances of residents being simply warehoused and receiving production-line treatment and medication, resulting in unwarranted and avoidable dire consequences.

Don't be defensive if a family elects to choose another physician. It may be the comfort or compatibility level of the resident or the family with the physician that makes a switch advisable. By the same token, don't hesitate to recommend another physician if you feel that a resident's personality or that of the family doesn't mesh with your own.

Physicians, you determine how you are respected at the facilities. If you overlook infractions and carelessness in others, or justify it in your own modus operandi, your integrity is at stake, as is that of the facility, not only with residents, families, and the general public but with those individuals within the system who strive to operate at their professional best. When you afford dignity to staff members and residents, your attitude and demeanor help set the tone for optimum conditions for all.

In giving public presentations on the prevalence of abuse in long-term care facilities, I strive to be entirely fair. I always try to make the point that there are good facilities, there are good physicians, and there are good nurses, CNAs and facility staffs. If we are all doing our jobs as we should be, why is there any need for defensiveness? How much abuse is allowable? How much neglect is tolerable? Can any abuse of fragile elders be acceptable?

One can be taught the science of medicine, but one must also learn the art of medicine. We don't expect you to be gods, but we do ask you to be "the physician." Think about why you became a physician. The medical profession is different from any other because of its power over life and death, and therefore carries responsibilities like no other profession.

Attention, please, physicians and medical personnel.

QUESTION:

What

would you have done

had this been

your mother?

Diane Sandell,
to Corporate Management

THIRTEEN

ATTENTION, PLEASE, ADMINISTRATORS AND CORPORATE MANAGEMENT

⌐ Attention, please, Mr. Chief Executive Officer, Ms. President of Long-term Care, Mrs. Administrator.

If you found yourself suddenly in the position of placing your loved one—Mom, Dad, Grandma—into a facility within two days, expecting dignified, quality care without exception, could you find it?

Of course! thinks Mr. CEO. One of our corporation's facilities. They're the finest in the industry.

Of course! thinks Ms. President of Long-term Care. But wait, there's that lawsuit pending.

Of course! thinks Mrs. Administrator. But wait—does that mean that I now have to worry about that new person I just hired?

Is there a place good enough for your mom, Mr. CEO? Do you really know your facilities?

Is there a place good enough for your dad, Ms. President? How many of your facilities received citations during the last inspection?

Is there a place good enough for your grandma, Mrs. Administrator? Are you careful enough about who works in your facility?

Families are apprehensive when they place a loved one in a facility. It's new to them. They're concerned. They've seen the disturbing TV programs. They've read the newspapers' graphic accounts of elder abuse. Still, they have to place Mother by Monday morning. They have to trust. They want to trust. Sometimes, they can trust.

There are well-run facilities that provide dignified, quality care. It begins with the administrator, who sets the tone for the entire operation.

She hires a highly qualified staff that meets her high standards. She senses their work ethic and their regard for the elderly. She oversees training, and interjects her personal expectations of excellence. Hers is a facility to be recognized, recommended, and emulated.

The facility where I moved my mother after her abuse exemplified these practices. (In fact, to be completely fair, my sister and I had, in the past, sent letters of commendation to the facility where the abuse later took place, citing specific instances of what we felt had been exemplary treatment.) From the first visit with the director of admissions, the positive atmosphere of the new facility was apparent in the gentleness with which they handled Mother, their providing the special bed, and the continuous nurturing by all staff to rebuild her sense of security.

It can be done!

Just as the administrator sets the tone for the facility, the CEO sets the tone for the corporation. Because this is a business specifically to care for our elderly, the responsibility and accountability for dignified quality care must begin and end with the CEO. Throughout the entire organization, from the executive officers to the facility staff, the CEO must determine, delegate, and demand compliance with expectations.

We need excellent corporations and facilities in business. We certainly want them to make a profit. As families and advocates, we surely want to work with the industry to assure this dignified, quality care. We appreciate those who do the job well. But you and I know, Mr. CEO, Ms. President of Long-term Care, Mrs. Administrator, that there are those who don't do the job well. There is neglect and there is abuse—to the point of death-inducing conditions—even in facilities considered top of the line. How can we tolerate this? When will we acknowledge the problem and determine to fix it? Let's do it now. It's in everyone's best interests: We are in a partnership—it's our responsibility.

The first step in solving any problem is to recognize and accept that there is a problem. Why can some facilities and corporations provide this care? Why can't they all? What will it take to accomplish this dignified quality care?

Corporate management personnel need to have information. How far up the chain and in what detail are reports of problems discussed? Mr. CEO, do you know? Anywhere along the chain of reporting, an employee protecting his job may fail to report an incident, make light of an incident, or make excuses for it. Aides tending to my mother the night of her abuse saw, but assumed her condition had been reported. The CNA in charge of her room claimed she did not abuse the resident, in fact purposely avoided her due to her verbal and physical abuse of the staff (an eighty-five pound, ninety-one-year-old strapped into bed).

There was no question in my mind that Mother had been beaten. I called the police, who came within the hour and investigated the case as "assault and battery." Three days later, the physician said the bruises could have been caused by a fall and by attendants picking her up. Licensing and Certification did not investigate for nearly a month, though there are clear regulations that suspected abuse must be investigated within twenty-four hours. Where did the system break down? There are many ways to circumvent accountability. Are we going to accept that? Don't you want to fix the areas causing the industry a bad reputation, costing the industry in insurance, fines, and defense fees, costing family trauma and sometimes even lives? These could be your parents!

CEOs and presidents, you need to be in dialogue with the ombudsman's office in each area where you have a facility. You need to be open to dialogue with families and advocates of residents. We urge you to engage in dialogue with the legislators in your state, speaking to their task forces about what it will take to solve the problem of providing the kind of care you want your parent to receive. Are you willing to consider an independent, objective troubleshooter, who reports directly to you, unbiased by direct involvement with a facility?

Corporations, as providers of long-term care, and CEOs, as the final authority, have a responsibility to ensure that the physicians practicing in the facility are of the same high quality you'd hire to look after your own mom. You set the standard and pass it down. Establish that overlooking neglect and abuse will not be tolerated. Establish that Medicare/Medicaid abuse (fraud) will not be tolerated. You know it happens. We know it happens. In northern California, indictments were brought against a physician specializing in geriatric medicine, and against the owner of a skilled nursing facility, totaling $4 million in false Medicare billings. In that district alone, fraud drains at least $1 billion a year out of the health care industry. (Reported in *The Sacramento Bee*, April 20, 1994.) Nor is the problem confined to any one district or state. Is it any wonder that the long-term care industry must contend with a bad reputation?

We ask administrators to live up to the impression given by the admissions office when interviewing to accept new residents. Continuing a dialogue with families and advocates who only want dignified quality care for elders brings us all into the partnership of responsibility. We've challenged families to inform themselves, to cooperate, to be responsible for their part in supporting their elder resident. We challenge administrators in kind.

We know there is the human element, involving so many people of differing histories, differing temperaments, differing care requirements, from both the resident's and the caregiver's side of the picture. We know there can be frustrations and aggravations on both sides of the bed rail. But please don't label a family as troublemakers when they are simply concerned about Grandma's welfare. Families do get frustrated when Grandma's dinner tray is plunked down out of her reach, grabbed up later when she still has not had a chance to eat, and her chart notes that she ate 80% of her meal. Why then has she lost twenty pounds in two months? What about your grandma?

Families do get frustrated when Dad's chair is wheeled down the hall so roughly and so fast that he cries out that his feet can't keep up and they hurt. What about your dad? Families do get frustrated when Mother is held over the toilet by two male aides, or left, uncovered, on her bed after returning from a shower. What about your mother? What about you, Mrs. Administrator? Can you truly defend these practices as acceptable and necessary?

Accept the responsibility when your staff doesn't do the job. When a mistake is made, admit it, correct it, and go forward. The needed correction might entail training; it might be a reprimand; it might be immediate dismissal.

We need to offer CNAs dignity and respect on the job. Theirs is the hands-on daily grind of caregiving. Without them the nursing home industry would fail completely. Let's investigate them well before hiring, fingerprint them for the corporation's assurance and the resident's protection, train them properly for the job, pay them well, offer incentives and bonuses such as a period of paid free time after a specified period of good service for jobs well done. With loyal staff feeling appreciated, absenteeism will be reduced, and you won't have to use temporary registry personnel so often. Use a suggestion box, available to staff, residents and families, for suggestions for improved services, and an appreciation box for recognition of work well done.

Because of the inevitable occasion of the death of a resident, and the typical three-shift schedule of staff, it is probable that one or more of the resident's caregivers will not be on the premises till the next shift change. Don't surprise these employees with a new resident already settled in the room. Establish some provision in the schedule at shift change to allow staff to acknowledge the loss before plunging into the routine of the new shift.

Make it easier for staff to report abuse without fear of losing their jobs. You are all mandated reporters. Families should be free to report abuse without fear of retaliation. Covering it up to protect the facility's "reputation" only leads to a poorer reputation. Instead, why don't we fix what's wrong so we can be proud of what's right?

Couldn't we all work together to respect the dignity of the residents and the staffs in our long-term care facilities? Some of the problems currently being experienced would not arise because they would already be taken care of. Isn't it worth it?

Consider this articulate poem by an unknown writer, found in her own handwriting in her bedside stand after she died in a nursing home.

Look Closer—See Me

What do you see, nurses, what do you see?
Are you thinking when you are looking at me—
A crabby old woman, not very wise,
Uncertain of habit, with far-away eyes,
Who dribbles her food and makes no reply
When you say in a loud voice, "I do wish you'd try."
Who seems not to notice the things that you do,
And forever is losing a stocking or shoe.
Who unresisting or not, lets you do as you will,
With bathing and feeding, the long day to fill.
Is that what you are thinking; is that what you see?
Then open your eyes, nurse, YOU'RE NOT LOOKING AT ME!
I'll tell you who I am, as I sit here so still,
As I live at your bidding, as I eat at your will,
I'm a small child of ten with a father and mother,
Brother and sisters, who love one another,
A young girl of sixteen with wings on her feet,
Dreaming that soon now a lover she'll meet;
A bride soon at twenty—my heart gives a leap,
Remembering the vows that I promise to keep;
At twenty-five now I have young of my own;
Who need me to build a secure, happy home.
A woman at thirty, my young now grow fast;
Bound to each other with ties that should last.
At forty, my young sons have grown and have gone,
But my man's beside me to see I don't mourn.
At fifty once more babies play 'round my knee,
Again we know children, my loved one and me.
Dark days are upon me, my husband is dead,
I look at the future, I shudder with dread,

For my young are still rearing young of their own,
And I think of the years and the love that I've known.
I'm an old woman now and nature is cruel—
'Tis her jest to make old age look like a fool.
The body it crumbles, grace and vigor depart,
There is now a stone where I once had a heart.
But inside this old carcass a young girl still dwells.
And now and again my battered heart swells,
I remember the joys, I remember the pain,
And I'm loving and living life over again.
I think of the years all too few—gone too fast;
And accept the stark fact that nothing can last.
So open your eyes, nurses, open and see,
Not a crabby old woman—look closer—SEE ME.

We challenge some corporation in the industry to be the trendsetter.
Mr. CEO, will you publicly state that there is a better way? Will you
publicly state that you are going to set the pace and turn this industry
around? Will you publicly state that you will initiate new criteria, new
standards, new education, new practices, and new, open communication? Will you publicly offer to share with other corporations and the
public what is working, what is making a difference? You would reap
the benefits of better care, better public relations, better employee
relations, fewer fines, lower defense fees, lower insurance rates—but
more than that, the knowledge that you could, with full assurance,
face any family member of any resident, and even your own mother.

Let's prove that it can be done and done well. Will you be the first?

Question: "Mr. CEO, what would you have done had this been your
mother?"

Answer: "Mrs. Sandell, I would probably have done exactly what
you are doing?"

And that's the bottom line.

Attention, please, administrators and corporate management.

*Government
is a trust,
and the officers
of the government are trustees;
and both the trust and the trustees
are created for the benefit of the people.*

Henry Clay
1829

⁂

*It is not enough for a great nation
merely to have added new years to life—
our objective must also be to add
new life to those years.*

John F. Kennedy
1963

Fourteen

Attention, Please, Legislators and Government Officials

꧁ Attention, please, legislators and government officials—Ms. Mayor, Mr. City Councilman, Ms. County Supervisor, Mr. Assemblyman, Ms. Representative, Mr. Senator, Ms. Governor, Mr. President—Mr./Ms. Any Official.

We do have laws about abuse of the elderly. But we still have a problem, a big problem, a silent problem, a city problem, a county problem, a state problem, adding up to a national disgrace. We don't want to talk about it. We don't want to read about it. Does that mean we don't want to do anything about it? It would seem so. It's difficult to draw any other conclusion.

Legislators, we know you are not law enforcement, and we don't expect you to be. But do you know the extent of the problem? Do you know what kind of elder abuse is going on in the long-term care facilities in your city? Do you know there is a way to find out? Do you know where you would place your mother if she suddenly needed to be in a skilled nursing facility and you had no one available to care for her at home?

Do you know the extent of elder abuse in your district or your state? Do you know what agencies regulate and oversee the facilities in your state? Do you know the procedures of the agencies regulating long-term care? What will you do when your dad cannot be cared for at home? Do you know how to find the best facility?

Do you know what percentage of the population of your state is in long-term care facilities? Do you know the incidence of abuse? Do you know the frequency with which certain facilities appear on investigation reports? Where will your older sister be placed if no one in the family can care for her? What about you? Any chance you might become a resident of a long-term care facility? Do you know what to expect there?

We recommend that all government officials visit the long-term care facilities in their own districts, to observe firsthand their constituents' care, and ascertain the answers to these questions.

I determined to tell my story to anyone and everyone who would listen. I felt that making people aware of the problem might be the first step in assuring that others would not have to suffer what my family went through. It has been an interesting and revealing odyssey. Although some encouraging steps have been taken, elders are still being beaten, intimidated, over-medicated, left unclothed while waiting for their showers, left in their own urine and feces, ignored and neglected. When are we going to get shocked enough or angry enough to do something definitive about it? Perhaps only when it happens to someone we personally love?

State Senator John Seymour heard my story and invited me to share it with his Senior Citizen Task Force. When he later went to Washington as a United States senator, an interesting turn of events led me to the office of California Assemblyman John Lewis, who was running in a special election for the vacated state senate seat. When I told a hesitant receptionist that I needed to see Mr. Lewis, and that I was determining how I would be voting the next day, she gave me an appointment.

I could not have been more pleased. Although there was the expected pandemonium in the office, Mr. Lewis listened attentively to my story and asked how he could help. I informed him about Senator Seymour's task force, and asked if he would consider establishing such a committee to keep him informed on issues affecting the elderly.

"Mrs. Sandell," he said. "If I am elected tomorrow, give me a call later and we'll discuss a task force."

He was and I did and we did! He later told me that if I would chair such a committee, he would sponsor it. (Details on establishing a task force are in Appendix H.)

In the following months, I was granted appointments with congressmen, senators, county supervisors, assemblymen, and various regulatory officials at local and federal levels. Because I went fully prepared and was considerate of their time, I was always received with respect, concern, and consideration.

We appeal to you elected officials. You were chosen by a majority of the voters. You have a responsibility to your entire constituency, even those confined in long-term care facilities. You have an opportunity to be a crusader for real improvement in the lives of the elderly—and won't we all be there someday?

You hold the key to the door to legislation that can make a difference. Please open that door. There are advocacies for birds, fish, whales, field mice, trees, wetlands, desert lands, wilderness lands, etc. In a nation that can send a man to the moon and beyond, why must our frail elderly fear for their dignity, their safety and even their lives?

Listen to constituents who ask to share their stories. We understand your busyness, but aren't your constituents' concerns your business? Grant just fifteen minutes. It can make a difference. Listen with an ear to informing yourself. Use the following suggestions to increase your knowledge and awareness, and then devote time to writing legislation to resolve these issues.

Don't assume that the cases you hear about are isolated cases. For every one who attempts to see you, many more are experiencing similar problems but don't know where to turn or how to ask for help.

Don't assume that the media give the whole picture. There is excellent coverage, and there is sensational coverage. Sensational coverage makes headlines for a day but is quickly forgotten. Excellent coverage attempts to provide correct information and awareness, but even that does not result in correction of the problems unless those with the interest, ability, and authority act on the information. Seek out more information. Subscribe to one of the advocate organization newsletters. Use a clipping service or create a volunteer one. Meet the ombudsman in your area and ask what, specifically, would help solve the problem. Establish a task force to gather information and make recommendations. Initiate a dialogue with representatives in other areas, perhaps encouraging a network of task forces for the purpose of coordinating information and possible legislation. With concerted, coordinated effort, maximizing volunteer task force personnel, innovative pilot programs might spotlight your district, your county, and your state, as the front-runner in the field of superlative elder care.

What about campaign contributions? Do you really know from whom you are accepting contributions? The long-term care industry invests heavily in electing legislators. Contributions are given through individual's names, which gives no indication of association with the industry. When corporation names are given they don't always reveal the field of the industry they represent. Why is the industry interested in supporting a candidacy? What do they expect in return? Will it have an impact on your decision-making? How do you feel about that? How might you feel if your parent had been severely beaten in a facility owned by a corporation in that industry?

What will it take to make a difference? It seems a harsh indictment, but we believe the only way things will change for the better, will be to make it too costly for the industry not to improve care. Some regulations are in place but if they are not enforced there is no incentive. Complaints may be processed, facilities investigated, cited with no fine, or citations of varying degrees of seriousness with (possible) fines. But fines are often waived because of various options open to the industry. *The CANHR Advocate* (the newsletter of the California Advocates for Nursing Home Reform, March 1996, Volume VI, No. 4, San Francisco, CA) reports:

"For the past ten years, nursing home advocates and consumers have witnessed the dilution of California's citation and fine system as it relates to nursing homes. Originally established to provide an enforcement incentive for poor performing facilities to comply with the laws, the system has gradually eroded to the point that fewer citations and fines are issued each year and few monetary penalties are collected...."

The industry sometimes charges that the advocacy groups are biased against it. But when we compare the viewpoint of the industry, which, understandably, must be operated for profit, with that of advocacy groups, many of which are staffed by volunteers working solely for quality care, where is the basis for a charge of bias? In that we simply want better care for our elderly, yes, perhaps we are biased. We want industry to do the job successfully, and profitably. We need successful, well-run facilities, and we'll need more in the future as our aging population grows. Let's cooperate to get the job done, and still provide dignified, quality care. Let's establish what needs to be done, determine what it will cost, and then find ways of providing funds to accomplish the task.

Many factors have excessively driven up the costs of providing quality care. We need to definitively end Medicare-Medicaid fraud, make those operators accountable, and initiate checks and balances that are not now in place. Freeing up monies misused through fraud and its defense could then provide more funds for proper daily care allotments.

There are several areas in which new or amended legislation would be helpful, both on state and national levels. Standardizing laws across the nation would simplify understanding and implementing protective measures.

1. **Fingerprinting**: California Senate Bill 945 (1998) requires fingerprinting of designated personnel: certified nurse assistants (CNAs), home health aides (HHAs), students enrolling in CNA/HHA training programs, and home health agency owners and administrators in virtually all facilities: skilled nursing, intermediate care, intermediate care for the developmentally disabled, home health agencies, nurse assistant and home health training programs, accredited nursing schools, general acute care hospitals, hospices.

2. **Notification procedures**: Current regulation in California requires skilled, long-term care facilities to report suspected abuse to the Department of Health Services—Licensing and Certification, and to notify either the ombudsman program or the local police department. That regulation should, in our opinion, require the immediate notification of both the ombudsman program and the local police department.

3. **Designations**: "Unusual occurrence." Unless the "unusual occurrence" designation is clearly defined, it removes the urgency from necessity to investigate immediately, because it depends on the description of the incident. According to California regulations, "unusual occurrences" must be identified and reported within twenty-four hours to the Licensing and Certification Department, where they are assigned a priority based on description of the incident. Patient abuse must be investigated within twenty-four hours, but the reporting and handling of an incident depends on the integrity of all personnel involved. In my mother's case, LCD did not investigate for nearly a month. We recommend the designation "unusual occurrence" be eliminated entirely in favor of a more definitive term, or amended by a mandatory further clarification of the nature of the "unusual occurrence."

Legislators and government officials, what can you do?

There are many possible recommendations. We recommend that legislators nationwide adopt legislative measures similar to California SB 679, The Elder Abuse and Dependent Adult Civil Protection Act, previously referenced in Chapter Seven, and California SB 945. Other protective measures are in effect in California and in other states. However, we feel the most important considerations would be interstate and national dialogue, the standardization of regulations throughout the nation, effective enforcement, and education of the public, in a clear, simple, standardized format, about the protective laws in effect. A publication for this purpose would be of the greatest community service.

Issue informed statements to the media, informing them that, like child abuse and spousal abuse, elder abuse cannot and will not be tolerated. Why do we even have to say that? When the long-term care industry understands that every area of government will take a proactive stand backed by legislation and enforcement to protect our nation's elder citizens, perhaps it will be brought to the "bargaining table" to solve these problems cooperatively, creatively, and productively without a defensive need to sweep things under the table. Let's work together to determine what it will take financially—without excuses, without waste, without fraud, without abuse—to provide dignified quality care for our elders, then determine how to make that happen.

What can one person in government do? What is your responsibility? Think about why you became a legislator. Pre-determine to do the right thing. Respond accordingly.

Attention, please, legislators and government officials.

What
wisdom can you find
that is greater than kindness?

Jean Jacques Rousseau
1712–1778

⚬

Shall we make a new rule of life
from tonight: always try to be
a little kinder than
is necessary?

James M. Barrie

FIFTEEN

EVALUATING YOUR ELDER'S CARE

No matter what you read or hear about the quality of life of America's senior population, it is difficult to know what to expect or plan for until you face a situation that affects you personally. Then you are emotionally involved and vulnerable.

The following five-step plan will help you assess your situation. It deliberately starts before placing a loved one in long-term care, but it can be adapted to situations arising both before and after placement. The key is creative problem solving. This plan is a "thought-starter" to help you walk through various circumstances you might be facing.

NOBLE FIVE-STAR PLAN FOR
EVALUATING AND IMPROVING ELDER CARE

You have begun to realize that your parent or other loved one needs more care. Whether he or she has been living independently and needs more assistance to continue, or has been living with you and is growing more dependent, roles are changing. The following five steps, discussed in detail below, will provide focus for evaluating the situation:

A. Assessing the Situation
B. Caring for the Caregiver
C. Learning the Resources
D. Making the Big Decision
E. Becoming Cooperative Partners With Long-term Care Facilities

A. Assessing the Situation

1. What is really happening here?

As your parent ages, there may be changes in personality that affect your relationship. Accept this new reality and don't take things personally. Try to seek positive and constructive solutions. Some personality changes respond well to medication and should be discussed with your physician. In some cases judicious use of certain medications can restore a sense of well-being and normalcy, extending the period of productivity and self-sufficiency in an elder's life. This is in no way a blanket endorsement of medication for mood adjustment—a practice too often overused to the point of abuse.

This can be one of the most frustrating seasons for the caregiver or decision-maker. The frustration is understandable. It is not wrong but simply a negative factor to be faced and resolved. Try to maintain calm. If possible take a breather, even if it's just a cup of tea. Irritation is contagious. It makes the elder more irrational and fearful. Use the suggestions in this plan to formulate your own plan for dealing specifically with your situation.

2. Who am I? Is my role parent or child?

Some, not all, elders lose their ability to make decisions, and may regress to childhood—a time when all their needs were met by others. You may begin to feel like the parent to your parent one day, only to find your parent back in control the next. Whenever possible, encourage your parent to make his own decisions, but be prepared to step in tactfully when necessary. Consider options ahead of time so that you are prepared to smooth over difficult situations. Getting caught off guard allows frustrations and irritations to build.

We call this the "dealing" stage, when deals or tradeoffs must be made to allow the parent to retain her dignity, with the protections of safeguards established by the caregiver. For example: If mom can no longer safely prepare meals at the stove, perhaps she can wash the vegetables for storage, help plan menus, make shopping lists, clip coupons, or fold grocery bags. If dad can no longer manage the check-book or the banking, perhaps an offer to help "translate that confusing bank statement form" would allow him to retain his dig-nity. Or invite him to read the ad pages for the best sales on something you need. If maintaining personal grooming becomes a problem, you might "deal" for an outing: "When you're finished with your bath, we'll go to the store (or the post office, the bank, the ice cream parlor, or take a stroll through the park around the corner)." The break will be good for both of you.

Sometimes the issue will be of greater importance. Dad may not be able to drive safely anymore. You cannot protect his dignity at the expense of someone else's life; you can, however, appeal to his sense of dignity at facing and making a right choice: "Dad, we love you. We don't want to chance losing you, and we know you don't want to be responsible for hurting someone else." Mom may not be reliable to baby-sit anymore. You cannot endanger her or your chil-dren for fear of hurting her feelings: "Mom, our friend Nancy is going to come play with the kids while we're out to dinner. I'll bet she'd like to learn some of your old children's songs to teach other kids she stays with." Dad may forget to take his medicine properly. Mom may imagine a threat to her safety—"seeing" people or things that aren't there. Issues of this nature must be resolved firmly but as gently and tactfully as possible.

3. Can I really handle what's going on? Do I need help? Will my family help? What do I do next? Where can I turn?

Only you can decide how much you are willing and able to handle. If there are other members of the elder's family, call a meeting to discuss options. Perhaps another relative would share some of the responsibility, take mom or dad for a month, a week, a day, or even just an outing. Or "sit" at your house while you get out for a lunch or dinner, shopping or a movie. Or share the expense of hiring a companion while you get away for a weekend. There are families in which this cooperative effort works well. There are families who won't even consider it, who won't offer a minute, or a dime, to help.

Remember that some family members simply cannot face certain types of deterioration in a parent's condition, and cannot force themselves even to relieve the caregiver. One daughter became so emotionally wounded by seeing her dad in a helpless condition that she could spend only minutes at his bedside, and put off visits for weeks. In this case the daughter-in-law became the caregiver, able to deal with the deterioration more objectively.

Only you can decide how much you are willing and able to handle. If you are carrying the responsibility for the care without assistance from others, clarify your own responsibility and commitment. If you have been designated as having the Durable Power of Attorney for Health Care (see Appendix C), you need not share the decision-making with those who do not share the physical, mental, or financial burdens. However, if there is a financial estate involved, family members who are unwilling to share the responsibilities may sometimes still attempt to influence or control essential decisions, or challenge your right to do so. An objective arbiter—a physician, a minister, or even an attorney—might be worthwhile and necessary to resolve differences. A Durable Power of Attorney for Health Care is strongly recommended, but requires early planning.

Only you can decide how much you are willing and able to handle. Within your immediate family, try to make the care of your elder a family undertaking if possible, sharing the work and responsibility as well as the fun, the sense of "family" and the rewards of knowing, loving, and serving your grandparent. There will be painful memories as well as good, but there can be a great heritage of family history and memories when it is truly a cooperative family effort. When there are tense times, allow family members to "own" their own feelings and reactions, even negative ones, with some ground rules regarding expression of those feelings.

Only you can decide how much you are willing and able to handle. Outside resources are available both for home care and for placing elders in care facilities. While these vary widely from city to city and area to area, you can help yourself by learning what your area offers in the way of support and assistance. (See Section C.)

4. Am I doing the right thing?

Regardless of how you elect to handle your situation, there will be people who think you should have done it differently. You must think through your emotions, abilities, resources, motives, strengths, and weaknesses honestly. Make the decision first in your own mind, and then with the significant others whose lives will be directly affected. Then smile graciously with no comment to those who disagree with your decision. Further discussion of all these subjects is covered in Chapter Sixteen, "Coping With the Dirty Dozen."

B. Caring for the Caregiver

I'm so tired. I'm not sure how much more I can take. I want to do the right thing for Mom. I want to keep Dad at home with us for as long as possible, but I'm so tired. Nothing I do seems to please Mom, and I'm so tired. Dad keeps repeating those stories of the old days over and over, and I'm so tired. Mother pouts when I try to keep her out of the kitchen, but she overflowed the sink last time. Then there was that skillet that nearly caught fire. I'm so tired. Dad can't understand that the boys want to play with their friends alone sometimes. Mom doesn't remember that children have to make noise sometimes. Oh, I'm so tired.

1. Is there help for me? Will they believe me? Will they understand?

Anyone who deals with elder care, whether in the home or in an institutional setting, will understand and believe what you have been going through. Fortunately, much more media attention is being given to the problems of elder care, and there is more awareness of the needs of the caregiver as well as the needs and problems of the elder. Early on, you can discuss the need for respite care with the primary care physician, who is likely to be aware of the need and to know some of the resources available locally.

2. Who can help? Whom can I trust? Will they be professional?

Many cities have senior citizen centers that can provide various types of diversionary help: adult classes, entertainment, therapeutic programs, and even day-trips for more active adults and day care supervision with activities for less active seniors. There may also be adult day health care centers that provide a wider range of services, including physical therapy, speech therapy, and other services for special needs. Some areas provide adult day care supervision without therapy. Many senior citizen centers can provide lists of available resources, such as paid companions or even volunteers who can provide you with a few hours of freedom to pursue your own interests. Many churches now offer this type of day care service to the community, and hospitals often have referrals for resources in the area. For your own reassurance, check into the sponsorship of these types of programs, just as you would for one of your children.

The diversions of such programs, for both the elder and the caregiver, are well worth the time and effort it takes to use them. Don't be discouraged by dad's hesitations or mom's complaints. The attention of and interaction with other people usually win over your reluctant senior, and you need the refreshment of time for yourself.

3. I need help right now. Who can help?

One of the best therapies for the caregiver is a good friend whom you can call when you need a break and a different perspective. This needs to be someone who understands your position and won't scold you for either your decision to care for your elder or your temporary weakness or frustration. It also needs to be a person who won't be turned off by your need for this outlet and will not discuss it with others. (The authors found such support in each other.) This is no place for an "I told you so." If necessary, agree to a few minutes for letting off steam, but then change the subject completely and talk about some interest you and your friend have in common—a book, a hobby, what's for dinner—anything to defuse the intense emotions brought on by your circumstances. Don't let it become a gripe session; the idea is to get your mind off the situation and give you a break from it.

If you are hesitant to burden a friend, find a support group. If you can't find a support group, start one yourself. (See Appendix I for suggestions.) Don't shy away from this vital source of encouragement. It can save your life.

4. Am I doing the right thing?

Anything you can do to increase the possibility of success in your venture is the right thing. Using community resources can give you just the break necessary to continue facing the situation at home. Don't be ashamed or afraid to reach out for help from the outside.

C. LEARNING THE RESOURCES

The feeling of being all alone in your situation can be your worst enemy. Educate yourself about all the possible resources for help, whether continuing to care for your elder at home or assessing the possibility of long-term facility care. Be a detective and a student. The following suggestions can get you started, but you may discover other resources. Network with everyone you can think of. Let them know your situation. You'll be surprised at the number of people who have similar situations and can offer suggestions and ideas.

Information Resources
•Family Physician • Hospital Geriatric Departments • Area Agency on Aging (terminology for these departments varies) • Ombudsman Program • Social Services Agency •Department of Health Services • Adult Protective Services

Disease-related Associations
• Alzheimer's • Parkinson's • Multiple Sclerosis • Cancer
Ask any of the above for referrals.

Support Systems
• Caregiver support groups and self-help groups
• Internet listings •Grass roots advocacy groups
• Ask hospitals, newspapers, churches, colleges
• Ask Senior Citizens Centers • Ask disease-related associations

Consider starting a support group (See Appendix I)
• Respite Care • Some hospitals and nursing homes maintain bed space for short-term care (vacation, illness, or crisis of caregiver)

Financial Assistance
• Private insurance (long-term care benefits)
• Medicare (hospital care, limitations on long-term care)
• Medi-Cal (in California) • Medicaid (in other states) • Family
• A conference of the elder's children (or other concerned relatives) to determine possibilities of participation in financial assistance

D. Making the Big Decision

When the time comes that you can no longer care for your parent's needs, in either your home or theirs, even with outside assistance, it is time to assess the options in facility care.

If your parent does not yet need a skilled nursing facility, assisted living facilities or residential care (board and care) facilities can be a pleasant, gentle transition into more controlled care. In a home-like atmosphere with other elders, there can be the sense of a family of contemporaries, the companionship of a generation in common. Some skilled nursing facilities also have resident-hotel type quarters where the residents have some freedom of movement and access but are under limited supervision.

Regardless of the type of facility, visit several, using the checklist offered in Appendix D to evaluate the quality of each. Try to find referrals from people you know and trust, but check them out personally. Contact the local ombudsman program for information regarding citations or fines from the state for neglect, or abuse, or other deficiencies. At any skilled nursing facility, yearly inspection reports should be posted and available on request. If a facility refuses access to this material, that fact should be reported to the ombudsman, and you should question whether that facility ought to remain on your list of prospects.

When you have narrowed the choices down to one or two, depending on your elder's ability to make an evaluation without becoming confused, take your elder to visit. Point out the pleasant aspects, the decor, the dining room, the companionship, the accessibility of medical care, and whatever else might appeal to your loved one.

1. Is this a decision my parent can make for himself, given the facts and choices?

If your parent is able to make a choice, the transition will be much smoother. It will be "her own" idea, and therefore more to be tolerated. Allowing that role in decision-making retains the elder's sense of control and choice and dignity in determining his future.

2. If my parent is unable to make the decision, am I willing to take that responsibility and commit to the follow-up necessary to ensure a smooth transition?

There may come a time when you must make the decision. If you make the choice for your parent, there may be times when he blames you for taking over, especially if he has difficulty adjusting to the new regimen. Be prepared to pleasantly stand by your decision, continuing to point out the benefits. Don't try to argue the point or defend your actions. Reassure your elder of your continued love and your understanding of her hesitancy.

If you have evaluated all the available facilities and have made the choice you feel is best based on all the factors, you may have to be prepared to accept your own decision despite your elder's objections.

3. Am I making the right decision?

Once again, only you can determine what is the right decision for you, your family, and your loved one. Not everyone—including your loved one—may agree with you. To provide the best chance of successful placement and subsequent care, we recommend using the following plan for a meeting with all personnel involved in the care of your loved one. While Section E below outlines the general objectives of the meeting, Appendix F offers a specific sample agenda, offering representative points for discussion, and suggestions for carrying out the meeting.

E. Becoming Cooperative Partners with Long-term Care Facilities

When the time comes to place an elderly loved one in a long-term care facility, it is important that the family, as the consumer, be knowledgeable and prepared to act in the best interest of the elder, hereafter called "resident" (not "patient") by standard industry usage.

Whether the need to enter a long-term care facility results from sudden trauma or comes after months or years of caring for the loved one independently, emotional and physical factors, such as misunderstanding, guilt, fatigue, frustration, and anger can make the family vulnerable to a sense of isolation and loss of control in this new environment.

The following plan was developed through NOBLE's involvement with many families. This concept provides a vehicle for families to exercise their "consumer rights" while assuring the long-term care facility of the family's cooperative intent. This plan consists of the family meeting with all the people involved in the resident's care, for purposes of outlining the expectations and planning the care. The better understanding resulting from this meeting provides better care for the resident from all points of view.

This meeting would take place before or during the placing of a resident; however, the concept could also apply to problem solving after placement. While a later meeting might take more planning and tactful, but emphatic, leadership, it could provide improvement in the quality of care.

We encourage families to help set the tone for the relationship between the family and the facility. Establishing this time for all who are involved in the resident's care to share openly and honestly—before any problems arise—allows for non-threatening, non-intimidating dialogue. When the resident's dignity, care, peace, and security are everyone's foremost purpose, the resulting atmosphere of cooperation benefits all.

The following is a list of those who should be involved in such meetings. The family should request and personally invite the representatives below. Full descriptions and functions follow.

1. Family member, caregiver, responsible party
2. Advocate for resident, other than family
3. Advocate for family, objective third party
4. Administrator of care facility
5. Medical professional (staff medical director, director of nursing, or resident's personal physician)

Scheduling this meeting for all to be present may be difficult; however, it is a reasonable request. If done with a professional attitude of optimistic problem solving, the facility should be amenable in light of the benefits for future cooperation.

1. Family member, caregiver, responsible party

The responsible family member, often the caregiver, should be prepared to discuss all aspects of care. This person is the most familiar with the resident's personal needs and habits, and can make helpful suggestions to the facility taking over the care. If the caregiver is too exhausted or stressed by the burden of previous care, the Family Advocate (#3) can take the responsibility of speaking for the caregiver. They should work together to prepare an agenda of points for discussion. List the points in related categories in order to contribute to an orderly, efficient meeting. This not only assures coverage of all items you wish to discuss, but allows the family to participate equally. Notes on this meeting should be recorded in the Care Journal mentioned in Chapter Eleven. Honor the time commitment of the others there by being knowledgeable and well prepared. (See Appendix F for a representative agenda.)

2. Advocate for Resident

This individual may be the local ombudsman, another family member, a friend, or a clergy person, someone whose only consideration is the objective caring for the expressed wishes and best interests of the resident. He/she can offer ideas from a viewpoint different from the caregiver's.

The ombudsman, available in all states, is an official representative to protect the interests of residents of long-term care facilities and to resolve problems and complaints. Because he/she probably is already familiar with the facility, this person may be a good choice to recruit as your resident advocate. At any rate, it is wise to get acquainted with this individual before you may need to request help with future problem solving. You can reach your local ombudsman by contacting your county's Area Agency on Aging.

3. Advocate for Family

This person represents vital support for the family member, and can be another family member or a friend. The individual must be a well-organized mediator with strong, tactful negotiating skills, able to clarify discussion of a specific point until mutually acceptable resolution is reached.

This person may be the most appropriate to lead the meeting if the caregiver is not a strong leader or needs moral support in this area. This individual should also make notes of the meeting points, any requested actions, etc., for follow-up and for a record of the discussions. These decisions should also be recorded in the journal.

4. Administrator of Facility

As the authority of the facility, this person has power to initiate action, balance your wishes and requests with the facility's rules and regulations, make necessary changes, and ultimately guarantee a satisfactory lifestyle for the resident. He/she sets the tone for all the facility staff. A spirit of cooperation for the benefit of the resident should be apparent.

5. Medical Professional

This may be the facility staff professional, medical director, director of nursing, or the resident's own physician. Request the presence of the medical professional, whose medical opinion, input, and consequent responsibility for treatment is vital to the success of the meeting as well as the care of the resident.

Thank God for tea!
What would the world do
without tea?—
how did it exist?
I am glad I was not born
before tea.

Sidney Smith
Lady Holland's Memoir

Sixteen

Coping With the Dirty Dozen

I've gone to look for myself.
If I should return before I get back,
Keep me here! —Anonymous

⧼ Who am I? Where am I? Learning to cope, to manage, to accomplish, to make do, to "hang in there," to persevere— these are the buzzwords of caregivers. Most caregivers have come to terms with the decision to be the caregiver, whether at home, in the elder's home, or overseeing care in a long-term care facility. The question is no longer whether, but how. In my personal experience and in most of the correspondence I received, most of the questions and frustrations of coping fall into twelve categories, which we choose to call the dirty dozen. Perhaps looking into each of the subjects in more detail will help you realize they are common to all of us, and offer you some relief and practical assistance.

1. Coping with Feelings and Attitudes

Feelings are sensory (products of the senses) and therefore responsive or reactive. Some are positive, some negative. Because they are real, they should be acknowledged, but they don't necessarily need to be expressed.

Attitude may be described as a mental outlook or position with regard to a fact. Attitude can, therefore, be conditioned by choice and self-control. Examples:

A. "Mom hurt my feelings with that remark."
Feelings: Hurt—the hurt is real.
Response or Reaction: Nursing the hurt, lashing out, pouting, justification.
Result: Potential for escalation of the situation to frustration, anger, hostility, lack of forgiveness, retaliation.

B. "Dad hurt my feelings with that remark, but… "
Attitude: The hurt is acknowledged but one's mental position, or attitude, tempers the response.
Response: Dad is hurting and frustrated by his inability to do all he used to do. I know he loves me and would not choose to hurt me. I choose not to accept the hurt.
Result: Not stuffing unacknowledged hurt beneath the surface, where it will fester and break out later, but choosing to hear the hurtful words through the filter of understanding the other person's frustrations.

What if mom, or dad, or auntie has always been hurtful, never expressing love or appreciation? If you have accepted the role of caregiver, you must choose, for the sake of your own wellbeing, to respond with self-control, with an attitude rather than by acting out feelings.

Author Pearl S. Buck has said, "You cannot make yourself feel something you do not feel, but you can make yourself do right in spite of your feelings." An attitude of choice includes choosing to love (love is a choice, not a feeling—See Paragraph 12), choosing to care, choosing to be kind, choosing to be gentle, choosing to respect, choosing to be patient—ah, that's hard, but patience, too, is a choice.

Rather like a successful marriage, it takes commitment. You can choose to make the relationship a success. Choose to make the parent feel welcome, wanted, loved, and honored. Choose to recognize and credit previous contributions, experience, accomplishments and family pride. Choose to be generous with praise for what the elder can do. Choose to overlook your negative feelings and those expressed by the elder.

If you "blow it" while trying to master this pattern of attitude above feelings, you aren't alone. If you lose your temper, choose to walk away from a volatile situation that could degenerate into abusiveness. Start fresh later. Choose to be the first to offer reconciliation if there is a problem, no matter where you think the fault or responsibility lies. No one gains when pride on either side builds cement walls where there should be gardens of understanding.

2. COPING WITH AWARENESS

You can ease or altogether avoid many problems associated with relationships with the elderly if you can learn to be aware of, and understand, changes in temperament or behavior. Sudden radical changes catch our attention immediately and confront us with the need to solve problems right now. However, many changes come so gradually that it's difficult at first to recognize any major difference in the personality. But if we are alert to what these changes might be, we then have time to explore the options open to us.

Helen's mother could converse with anyone about art or the latest book she had read, but thought her son-in-law was her own husband, and accused Helen of trying to steal him from her.

Will's father-in-law could still create beautiful wooden toys, but when Will offered to help him straighten out his hopelessly confused checkbook, he told all the neighbors Will was trying to steal his money.

Jody's friends saw her mother as a delightful and entertaining luncheon companion, hardly believing Jody's frustrations with mom's fears and constant complaints. When Aunt Marie stood at the bathroom mirror studying her reflection for long periods of time instead of washing her face and brushing her teeth, Nancy thought auntie was vain and purposely delaying leaving the house on errands. When auntie was later diagnosed with Alzheimer's Disease, Nancy learned that the disease sometimes robs its victims of the ability to think through simple daily tasks of personal grooming.

Caregivers who give love and time and effort, often sacrificing personal comfort and privacy to help their elders, frequently report such situations among their most frustrating times. Many report guilt when they later realize mom's fears were legitimate to her, and dad's cantankerousness was brought about by frustration with his own diminishing capabilities. "If only I had known!" is the cry of many caregivers who might have been able to respond with more understanding and compassion had they been aware that the elder is not always in control of unusual behavior.

Becoming aware of potential problem areas before they arise can defuse frustrations that lead to conflict. Before reacting to a personality quirk, consider whether it might be related to the elder's own fear or frustration, or even a change in physical or mental ability.

Changes in an elder's attitude and behavior are commonly noticed in many areas: Mom becomes forgetful, misplaces and hides things, neglects her appearance, personal hygiene, and usual activities and duties, becomes abrupt and demanding. Dad becomes reclusive or demands inclusion in every activity, has unusual fears and obsessions, becomes suspicious and accusatory, uses unacceptable language, forgets social restraints and courtesies, loses understanding of money-handling, changes eating habits, sleeps too much or too little, wanders, snoops, doesn't respect privacy.

The list goes on and on. You could add your own observations. The point is to increase your own awareness of changes, in order to be prepared to respond with levelheadedness and understanding. Even when you don't really understand, it's important to keep your own dignity and that of your elder intact. (The dignity of the caregiver is discussed in Paragraph 11.)

3. Coping with Family Involvement

A discussion of family involvement in caregiving was presented in Chapter Eleven, "Attention, Please, Families." However, even with the best of intentions and the best of plans, there will still be times of frustration and conflict. The ideas presented here primarily affect the role of the caregiver's family when the elder is living with the family.

The commitment to caring for an elder at home should take into consideration the needs of the immediate family, but the decision-makers—the caregiver (and spouse, if applicable)—must make the final decision. All members of the family need to understand it is a decision you are choosing to make, even if you feel you have no other choice, and could be a long-term decision. Save yourself the frustration of re-hashing arguments about whether the decision should have been made. Adjustments and compromises will be necessary. Schedules will not be as easily established or changed as before. Attempt to "be there" for your children's activity schedules, but help them learn the give-and-take of balancing wants with needs. Spontaneity to pick up and go will be curtailed. Establish a ground rule specifying that only positive problem solving discussions take place. Recruit the kids' creative suggestions.

Sometimes, you will have to make unpopular decisions. Try to maintain an open, cooperative atmosphere, where the children learn the value of teamwork and compromise. Offer flexible terms of negotiation, but see that negotiations are carried out as quickly and equitably as possible. Don't trap yourself in promises that can backfire, just to ease the immediate situation. Be realistic.

4. Coping with Responsibility

In Chapter Eleven, "Attention, Please, Families," we discussed the need for mutual understanding and settling the issue of responsibility for the care of the elder within the extended family. Assuming that the role of caregiver has now come to you and your immediate family, it may be necessary to further assess and clarify within that unit to deal with the ever-changing circumstances requiring decisions.

As far as is possible, allow your loved one to retain as much responsibility for himself as he is able. My dad was able to handle the business aspects of his life—checkbook, banking, insurance, and appointments—and retain the dignity of continuing in that role. However, unfamiliar or unexpected details panicked him. For instance, Medicare statements outlining treatments and providers of services look like, but aren't, bills. In Dad's mind, these were bills that had to be paid immediately, and he worried whether there was money to cover them. Other caregivers report that advertising materials for goods or services also look like bills because they include order blanks. Health fund drives, broadcasting fund drives, religious fund drives, unsolicited "gifts" of stamps, calendars, stationery, etc., all tend to appeal to loyalty and generosity, and are easily misunderstood.

Allow mom to make as many choices as possible in determining her welfare. She may choose a dress you don't care for, but if she loves it and it makes her feel good, and it isn't inappropriate, don't impose your choice on her. Just because she needs physical assistance in living arrangements, don't assume that she's unable to make other decisions with wisdom and experience. There may come a time, because of diminished understanding or capability, when you must take over responsibilities your loved one previously handled for herself.

One dad, in complete control of his mental faculties before a major surgery, resisted, but finally reluctantly signed a power of attorney enabling a trusted daughter to handle his business matters if necessary during his recuperation. A stroke immediately following the surgery left him unable for the rest of his life to speak, write, or even indicate his opinions.

Offer your assistance tactfully, as a benefit, not a seizing of control. It is wise to have previously arranged for alternate signatures on a bank account or a power of attorney, which allows the designee to handle business affairs. But, as described above, this is a touchy subject, which many elders have difficulty accepting. Unfortunately, it is also an area in which financial abuse of the elder can occur. Perhaps an objective friend or advisor, trusted by the elder, can help explain the benefits of prearranging the handling of business. Always place yourself in your loved one's position. *What if this was happening to me?* Reassure your loved one that this measure simply allows you to help him/her through the often-confusing aspects of financial matters.

Some concerned elders want to talk about death and final arrangements. We sometimes shy away from the subject, thinking we are reassuring them of long life—"Oh, Mom, you're going to live forever"—when our own hesitancy to talk about the subject of death of a parent is the issue. Many elders know their time is becoming limited, and they need to settle the issues now. Be prepared to accept their reality. In so doing you will give them the gift of peace of mind, and you will learn details that will help you make those final arrangements when the time comes.

5. Coping with Role Reversal

"Sarah, I'm hungry. When's dinner? What's for dinner?"

"Mother, we just got up. Breakfast will be ready in a few minutes."

"I don't want breakfast. It's dinnertime. I don't like eggs."

"But, Mom… "

"Well, I'm not having breakfast. I'm not going to eat."

What's going on here? She's behaving like a child? Am I her mother?

Does role reversal really happen? You bet it does, and it can throw you for a loop till you realize what's happening. We fight against giving up the nurturing we ourselves still want, in order to nurture this vaguely familiar child in our parent's body.

As long as our parents live, we still want and expect them to be our parents. The unexpected slipping from one role into another catches us off guard and keeps us on edge.

I don't know if I can handle this. Where's my Mom? Who am I supposed to be?

I need my mom.

But your mom may be there the next morning, hungry for eggs again. The first evidence of role reversal isn't always permanent, but it can be a sign of what's ahead. The frustration occurs in that slippery time of never knowing which role mom is in at any given moment. Like the Boy Scouts, you feel you always have to "Be prepared." The frightening thing is that you don't know what to be prepared for. What's next? Eggs and breakfast aren't so hard to deal with, but next time, mom may head down the road looking for her Mama. Then what?

At this point of recognizing role reversal, we actually begin the grieving process of separation associated with death. Our parent is no longer as we knew him/her. It isn't easy, but now is the time you must accept what is and move on to what must be. You must begin to accept your new role of providing the care and nurturing and making the decisions associated with being a parent to this loved one.

Sometimes you'll make the right decision. Hooray! Relish it. Remember it. Try it again. It may or may not work the next time. If it doesn't, don't punish yourself. You are in trial and error territory. Be kind to yourself.

6. Coping with Dignity

Retaining the elder's dignity is probably the most important thing you can do for the loved one under your care. It may take some creative thinking, but choosing to make it a priority will go a long way toward preserving the success of your relationship.

The current trend toward idolizing youth, beauty, and fitness has left many of our elders not only without dignity and honor, but without advocates as well. Elders facing new living arrangements, giving up their own homes, moving to a retirement center, an adult child's home, or a long-term care facility, have fragile egos and feelings. Whatever the reason for the change—illness, enforced retirement, diminished capabilities—the need for the radical change in their lifestyle usually results in a traumatic assault against already vulnerable sensitivities. Mother may have been a very capable business executive before retirement sneaked up on her, leaving her feeling useless. Dad may have been a strong, vigorous outdoorsman used to outwitting nature at every turn, before a stroke left him unable to step out the back door without assistance.

Dignity should be a given in every person's life, but unfortunately it is not. Dignity should mean free choice, freedom from embarrassment, freedom from mental, physical, and fiduciary abuse, regard and respect for each individual as a human being regardless of his condition.

In a long-term care facility, my mother was occasionally bathed and taken to the bathroom by a young male aide her grandson's age. This was impossible for her to accept, but she had no choice. She was dressed and undressed without the privacy of a curtain or closed door. She had no choice. She was confined in a wheelchair for too long at a stretch. She had no choice. Her bathroom was not checked for cleanliness often enough. She had no choice. She often had to wait too long to be taken to the bathroom, or to be changed if she had an accident. She had no choice. She was handled roughly, with evident bruising. She had no choice. Her personal belongings, even her dentures, disappeared. She had no choice.

While these examples happened in a long-term care facility, indignities can sometimes occur in our own homes when we get too busy and too rushed or too tired and overworked to feel empathy with the one we're caring for. We cannot teach dignity, just as we can't teach love and caring, but we must require accountability for common courtesies. The accumulation of small indignities can also be powerful in eroding a person's sense of well being and control over his own life, resulting in shattered self-respect, withdrawal, and depression.

During the time my mom and dad lived with us, there was a period in which I also nursed my husband's father during what turned out to be his final illness. He was a proud man who hated the condition his illness had brought on him. He was used to being in control of his life, and it was difficult for him to accept anything in the way of personal care from me. I had grown up knowing, respecting, and, finally, loving him, and I didn't want anything to interfere with that mutual respect. As the days went by, I became more uncomfortable with his obvious discomfort with what I had, of necessity, to do in caring for him. I tried to start each morning on a happy note but it became harder to create one-sided pleasantries as the days went by.

One morning, as I opened the draperies to let the sunshine in, I spontaneously said, "Good morning, Sam. It's a beautiful day." I wondered where that came from. His name was Alwyn, but I called him Grandpop. There was no visible response, but I felt better, so the next morning I tried it again, with a chuckle in my voice. Still no response. Because it lightened my mood, I said it again the third morning as I opened the draperies.

"Good morning, Samantha," said a teasing voice from the bed. I nearly fell over. That became our greeting every morning, and though it served to lighten our relationship and our daily activities, I realized that it also created an atmosphere of nurse to patient, instead of daughter-in-law to father-in-law, which eased the embarrassment of the nursing care. I loved him all the more.

Retaining and reinforcing personal dignity can be one of the most powerful therapies you can offer your elder. Make it your choice! As a resulting benefit, you, too, will experience the strengthening of your own dignity.

7. Coping with Idiosyncrasies

There is a story of a young bride who carefully and neatly cut a piece off each end of a ham before placing it in the roasting pan for the oven. Puzzled, her new husband asked her why. "Because Mom always did it that way," was the reply. The next time the young couple visited her parents, they asked her mother about the ham preparation. "My mother always fixed her hams that way," was Mom's answer. Finally, at Christmas, the entire clan gathered at Grandma's old farmhouse. Sure enough, Grandma prepared a ham, slicing off each end of the meat before placing it in the roasting pan. "Grandma," the young bride asked, "I've asked Mom and she doesn't know. Why do we have to cut off the ends of the ham before baking it?" Grandma laughed and pointed at the pan with her knife. "I don't know why you and your Mom cut off the ham. I do it because my pan isn't big enough to hold the whole thing!"

Eccentricities, oddities, peculiarities, habits, quirks—we all have them, and not necessarily because we're old. I always have to make the bed before leaving the house. Just have to. Even if we're late. My husband teases me that if we were ever burglarized at least the robbers would see the bed was made. It just so happened that we were burglarized once. I don't make light of it because it was a frightful thing to walk into the house and see things strewn about. But wouldn't you know it that happened to be the one time in thousands that the bed wasn't made. Some idiosyncrasies are endearing, some are weird, and some are irritating, especially when they're someone else's. And when we're facing the other aspects of caregiving, and dealing with the mysteries of aging personalities, they can become the "straw that broke the camel's back."

Telling the same stories over and over and over. And over! (Till you know the stories and remember the names, dates, and incidents better than the one telling it, and are tempted to break in to finish the story.)

Asking the same questions over and over and over. And over!

Fixing the sofa pillows or folding the napkins just a certain way.

Saving things: rubber bands, plastic margarine cups, pencil stubs, used plastic bags, broken shoestrings.

Draping wet dishtowels all around the kitchen; ironing clean dishtowels.

Hurrying to get the mail before anyone else can.

Washing paper plates to use again.

Idiosyncrasies are as individual as the people who have them, and we all have them. If we try to understand or figure them out or change them we run into frustrations. If they are just harmless quirks, allow the elder to "own" his own idiosyncrasies.

Consider the impact over time. Does it really matter, in the long run, whether dad saves rubber bands or mom washes paper plates or drapes wet towels around the kitchen? You can discreetly gather laundry or dispose of the paper goods later. There is a popular slogan: "Don't sweat the small stuff. (It's all small stuff!)" But caregivers know it isn't. If Grandma loses the mail or hides important things, other solutions need to be found. On one of the last visits to her mother's home, Elaine observed Marie leafing through a two-foot stack of old magazines till she finally pulled out a twenty-dollar bill to take shopping. After Marie was hospitalized with a stroke, and it was known she would never be able to live at home again, Elaine and her sister were cleaning out the apartment. Remembering Marie's unusual "banking system," the girls leafed through the stacks of magazines and found seventy-two dollars.

8. Coping with Fear

Many idiosyncrasies stem from fear: fear of change, fear of the unknown, fear of losing control of one's own life, fear of losing one's health, fear of death.

Sitting up all night for fear of dying in bed.

Scotch-taping the curtains to the wall all around the window "so no one can peek in."

Refusing to eat because "someone is trying to poison me."

Becoming suspicious, argumentative, uncooperative: "they're whispering about me," when, in reality, the elder denied being deaf and refused to consider a hearing aid.

My mother had a terror of being buried alive. In her childhood she had heard of a person, thought dead, who awoke and sat up in the mortuary. I repeatedly promised her that we would not allow her body to be prepared for final disposition until three days after she died. We kept that promise. Although I was embarrassed to make the request of the funeral director, he accepted it as Mom's wish and our promise, and he graciously fulfilled the request.

Gently and repeatedly addressing the fears with affirmation and a loving, caring attitude may help restore confidence. Caregivers, overworked and overtired, may have difficulty hanging on to patience. Try to see the person through the eyes of her own fears. Realize that rational thinking probably is not possible. It's hardest when the accusations and suspicions are directed at you, the caregiver, or a member of your family. Although the suspicions and accusations directed at me stung, I could overlook them. But when Mom turned on my husband, who had shared in caring for her for twenty-five years, I confronted her and attempted to make clear that this was untrue and could not be tolerated. Nothing I said could convince her, and this was the beginning of the end of my ability to care for her at home.

If you suspect that your loved one's level of fear might indicate paranoia of psychotic proportions, which is not uncommon, you should inform your physician. Medication can, at times, be very effective in reducing this symptom (disturbing to both patient and family), and can make the difference between safely staying at home, or institutionalization.

You can't be prepared to recognize and ease every fear that may assail your loved one beneath the veil of who she's become. It's not really what you say to alleviate her fear; it's the way in which you address her, your tone of voice, your quiet manner. It's a continuous job of reassurance, for which there is no preparation. You just have to keep reinforcing, and know that it's probably going to get worse.

Your elder's fears may seem trivial and therefore strain your patience, but every single fear is very real to your loved one and, from her viewpoint, needs to be addressed right now! It takes patience, persistence, and love, even when you don't feel like it. See Paragraph 12, regarding "love when you don't feel like it."

The result of not addressing her fears is an agitated, frightened, angry, hurt, fearful, human being. Sometimes, all that's needed is for the elder to see you making an attempt to remove the fear. When all else fails try a hug. If the hug doesn't work, then just be there so she's not alone at the moments when she's most afraid.

9. Coping with Frustration

Frustration is probably at the root of all coping problems. Frustrations are inevitable, but how we deal with them determines the climate of success we create in dealing with our aging loved ones. When we're raising our children, we all have a tendency to want to "make it all better." In the same way, when we find ourselves parenting our parents, we want to make all their problems and frustrations disappear. But we can't make everything all better. We can't change the elder's reactions to exasperating situations, but when we change our expectations of them and of ourselves, we can ease the tensions surrounding the problems.

Usually, frustration results from thwarted desires, plans, or expectations, or a clash of differing wills, personalities, or methods of problem solving. It's a creative challenge to resolve problems with increasing frequency and decreasing frustration. Keep in mind that easing your elder's frustration level also eases your own.

Humor can defuse many tense situations. One caregiver reported that after months of frustrating turmoil in the household, with everyone in the family at odds with one another, they finally realized that her mother-in-law was playing one member of the family against another, constantly agitating. Then she'd go off to her room and shut the door. They recognized that her temperament was not likely to change. Understanding her disposition helped them not to react with one another, and gentled their reactions to her. They were able to turn it into a private family joke with each other, saying, "Grandma's not really happy till everyone else is in an uproar."

I like to use the analogy of a box tied up with ribbon, sitting on your closet shelf. I suggest you actually prepare such a box. Make it a pretty one with lovely ribbon. When you're faced with frustrations you aren't yet prepared to solve, take some time out, write the situation on a piece of paper, place it in the box and tie the bow. Tightly! Writing it down, frustration and all, relieves some of the tension and articulates your feelings. Placing it in the box prevents the psychologically dangerous reflex of "stuffing" your feelings internally, only to have them erupt later, unsolved and more damaging. Instead, when you feel calmer, take down the box, untie the bow, take out one of your written frustrating situations, and evaluate it.

What about this situation frustrates me? Thwarted desires, plans, or expectations? Are my desires and plans legitimate? Is there any other way I can accomplish my goals? Do I expect too much of Mom? Of myself? Is it a clash of personalities or wills? Were we always like this? Why does this situation frustrate me? Am I trying to prove something? Is there something from our past relationship that I'm trying to get even for? Am I getting some reward from trying to prove a point with this dear old soul who used to do so much for me? Or maybe she didn't do so much for me. Is that why I'm frustrated? Am I punishing her for a perceived lack in our shared past?

Try putting yourself in your loved one's shoes. As an exercise, try stuffing your ears with cotton or covering your eyes. Try using only the left side of your body, as if the right side was paralyzed from a stroke. Try sitting upright in a hard chair for a period of time. When you need to go to the bathroom, consider what it would be like if you had to wait forty-five more minutes for help. Think about what it's like to have an aide of the opposite sex undress you before you go to bed at night. Consider your loved one's frustration at not being in control of his own life. Consider her fear of the unknown. Is there something you can do to alleviate those fears and frustrations? A soothing word, a smile, a gentle touch, a bit of the "golden rule," a capitulation to his/her way of wanting to do things, or something even more tangible—a change of plans to really make mom feel like "Queen for a Day." Just once in a while—would that be so difficult?

Evaluate the options. Jot them down. Now place your note back in the frustration box and tie the ribbon back around it. Try the new ideas for a few days. Think of it as a gift you are willing to offer your loved one. Think of the beautiful ribbon. Smile a lot.

You may never get to all the frustrations in the box, and that's okay. And some days you may not even have time to physically write down the situations. The box can be symbolic. Do it mentally. Choose to lay it aside. The benefit comes from freeing yourself of the unnecessary baggage. You can get on with today, with the promise that, like Scarlett O'Hara—I'll think about it tomorrow.

This is not procrastination; this is survival. Face it and solve it when you can, but perhaps some of the frustrations will cease to be frustrations when the pressure is taken off.

10. Coping with Guilt

How do I feel guilty? Let me count the ways.

A. Roy feels guilty because he had to place his mother in a long-term care facility against her wishes.
B. Ellen feels guilty because she couldn't take care of Roy's mother in their home.
C. Sarah feels guilty when she goes out to lunch with a friend without taking her mom along.
D. David feels guilty when he visits his widowed mother, who still lives in her own home. He visits twice a week but feels he should go more often.
E. Elmer feels guilty for shouting at his son to hurry, when it was Grandpa who was so slow getting to the car.
F. Laura feels guilty for asking her fifteen-year-old son to share a room with his six-year-old brother to make room for Grandpa.
G. Angie feels guilty for wanting to run out of the room when her mother starts complaining about the children's noise in the afternoon when Grandma wants to nap.
H. Susan feels guilty for shutting the door to her bedroom when she and her husband retire for the evening.

And the list goes on, and on, and on. You get the picture.

Every caregiver has grappled with guilt—real guilt and false guilt. Every caregiver must learn to deal with both. There is no room for either. There is no excuse for either. Now, doesn't that make you feel guilty?

Take a "True-False" test. Re-read the list above and mark each one T for true guilt or F for false guilt.

Now let's look at the examples in more detail.

A. After considering all the options for his mother's necessary level of care, Roy has made the only choice possible. Even though his mom doesn't like the decision, he has no reason to carry guilt.

B. Ellen works full-time, has two busy teenagers, and has never had a close relationship with Roy's mother. She has no reason to carry guilt.

C. Sarah is a homemaker caring for her mom at home. They are together daily. She needs time to "be Sarah" with her own friends, and not just "daughter Sarah." She has no reason to carry guilt.

D. David is single, an only child who feels responsible for his mother since his dad's death. He travels a lot in his business, but still manages to see Mom twice a week. Yet every time he sees her, she verbalizes her wish that he'd come more often. It is probable that her complaint would be the same whether he came more, or less frequently. David has no reason to carry guilt.

E. Elmer is frustrated with Grandpa, and though he would not shout at his father, he thinks that by yelling at his son, Grandpa will get the point. The guilt he feels is true guilt, but can quickly be eliminated when Elmer apologizes to his son for taking his frustration out on him. Of course, this does not give Elmer license to shout at Grandpa instead. He might alleviate the problem by exercising "creative timing"—allowing more time than necessary to get to their destination, or giving Grandpa an earlier departure time than actually needed so Grandpa doesn't feel rushed.

F. Sometimes families simply have to learn the give-and-take of shared living quarters, provided that is the best or, perhaps, only option. If, instead of feeling guilty, Laura could put her energies into creatively adapting the available space, several valuable lessons about responsibility might result. (See more detailed discussion in the previous section on Family Involvement, #3 above). Creative room division, involving her sons in the planning, establishing "ground rules," making appropriate concessions to her older son, all might create a better atmosphere, but Laura need not carry guilt for doing what is necessary for Grandpa's care.

G. Angie feels trapped by a repetitive behavior that is unlikely to change. It is reasonable that Grandma needs a nap. It is also reasonable that children are sometimes noisy. Flexibility is a sanity-saving asset. A quiet time for Angie and the kids could become a precious time out for crafts or projects, board games, reading together or separately, taking a trip to the library, the park playground, or any other activity or "field trip" that would give Grandma time for a nap. Conversely, Grandma, with more available discretionary time, might be persuaded to nap at another time, and might need to realize that in a home with small children there will sometimes be noise. Angie does not need to carry guilt about children being children, nor put guilt on them as long as reasonable courtesies are observed.

H. In a shared living situation, the elder is not a guest to be entertained. Susan and her husband need time alone together. She need not feel guilty for shutting the bedroom door and, if necessary, installing a lock and using it.

Of the examples given, only E represents true guilt. True guilt is for something, whether intentional or unintentional, that has caused hurt, or pain, or hardship. False guilt is guilt you assume for things that are not your responsibility or in your power to change.

Now make a list of all the things you've been feeling guilty about. Examine your guilty feelings and try to identify the source of each. Mark a T or an F by every item on your list. If you evaluate your list objectively, most of the things on your list are probably false guilt. Mark a line through all the things on your list that are false guilt. Determine to dismiss them, and refuse to pick them up again. Now look at the remaining items. If there are reasons for true guilt, determine an action to make them right. Is an apology needed? Do it. Is there something that can be done to alleviate the situation? Do it. Now, or as soon as possible. Then forget it and end it. Make the decision and the choice to set things right.

No guilt should last longer than it takes to identify its authenticity and deal with or dismiss it. That's a tough assignment, but it can be done. For your own sanity, do it.

11. Coping with Caring for the Caregiver

Caregivers are often multi-multi-functional. You've seen the lists of professional tasks that "ordinary" women perform: housewife, career-woman, mother, nurse, chauffeur, errand-runner, tutor, secretary, chef, entertainer, companion, lover, cleaning lady, laundress, seamstress, and so on. When a man becomes the primary caregiver, and the numbers are increasing, he is not exempt from the multiplicity of responsibilities, many of which are listed above. Add all the duties of caring for an older generation (again, whether at home or in long-term care), and you see that many caregivers feel they can never stop for a break or see to their own legitimate needs. You sometimes feel, mistakenly, that you're indispensable. It is a formidable undertaking, but like any efficient piece of machinery, proper upkeep and maintenance is a must. You have got to take care of you. You owe it to yourself; you owe it to your family; you owe it to your elder.

As discussed in the previous paragraph, deal with guilt. If you are the caregiver, don't let anyone else lay guilt on you, and don't lay it on yourself. If another family member is the primary caregiver, help that person not to assume guilt.

Determine the areas in which you yourself need nurturing—physical, mental, emotional, and spiritual. Make lists of things that minister to you in each area. Separate the lists into categories depending on the chunks of time necessary to accomplish them, from five minutes to a whole weekend away. Find ways to work the smaller pleasures into your day, every day.

As with small children, use the time when your elder is napping to do things for yourself. Take a long bath, do your nails, read a book, sit in the sun or the shade and listen to the birds, make lemonade, or take a nap. Go out to the garage and putter if this is a pleasure for you.

Polish your car or your golf clubs, work on a project, read a book, pull a few weeds, if this is therapy for you, and not a chore. Do not do the laundry or scrub the bathroom, or take out the trash. There will be time for that. For now, treat yourself.

When you're feeling shredded from the constant calls for your attention, it may be necessary and appropriate to respond, "I'll be there in just a minute (or five)." Then, when you can reasonably break into what you're doing, attend to the elder's request, but don't abuse this "grace period" of delay.

There may be several ways to take a break away from home. Sue, with a fairly active elder, found another caregiver with an active elder and they traded mornings, bringing the elders together to visit, or sit in the park, or go for a drive while the other caregiver had a break. Lois tried a similar routine and found it was more trouble for her than it was worth. It took more time to get her elder ready and out; it didn't seem to entertain the elder and it added stress to Lois' day to include another person to look after for even a short time. Janet's sister, who worked during the week, agreed to come every other Saturday morning so Janet and her husband could go out to lunch together.

It won't all be positive. One desperate caregiver arranged, at considerable expense, a weekend at a board and care for her Mom while she and her husband had a weekend (also at considerable expense) at a favorite place within easy driving distance. The first evening, they luxuriated in the privacy, the pool, and the lovely restaurant. Then she found herself crying all the second day as she realized she had to go home the third. She was also worried about how her mom was handling the weekend. She tried to laugh at herself for crying, but realized she'd waited too long to take the break.

We've discussed extended family involvement in Chapter Eleven, "Attention, Please, Families." However, if there is extended family, other children or grandchildren of the elder, it may be wise to initiate a specific request, and specify a time. Don't wait for someone to volunteer. You may be met with a refusal; if you can't negotiate a compromise, you need to learn to accept that without bitterness. Check the resources offered in Chapter Fifteen, "Evaluating Your Elder's Care," for assistance in finding paid companions or even volunteers to help free you for your own respite.

Don't make yourself or your family ill by holding in the difficulties. Share with someone you trust, an understanding friend, or even a professional, someone who is not involved personally. Make an appointment with dad's doctor or a clergy person, for a private time when you can perhaps get some insight into your situation, and learn positive approaches to solving problems.

It may seem obvious, but it's often overlooked—keep yourself well groomed. When you feel you're shut in at home with your elder, it's easy to let personal grooming slide. How many of us have been caught answering the door looking unkempt? It's an old adage, but true, that when you look your best you feel better. We've already discussed the psychological advantages of helping the elder maintain good grooming, but it's true for the caregiver as well. Not only do you feel better, but also you project an image of calmness and self-control.

Bottom line? You are not only caregiving for the elder but also for the caregiver—you. You deserve it. You will function more efficiently and more serenely when you nurture your own needs—physical, mental, spiritual, and emotional. Even taking this into consideration, there will be days when you feel put-upon and martyred. You have already discovered there are daily ups and downs. On days when everything goes well, the residual "fallout" refreshes everyone. There will be dark tunnel days when nothing seems to work and there is no light anywhere. Try to dismiss them. Don't carry hurts and grudges to bed, where they will nag you and rob you of rest and peace of mind. Learn the art of doing what you can and releasing the rest.

12. COPING WITH LOVE

Do you have to cope with love? Coping sounds like a burden. Isn't love a given? My own feeling was that love is a natural, a given, because I was always surrounded with it and I loved both my parents deeply. My mom loved every kid who ever came through our door, and there were always cookies, "one for each hand," for each kid. I can still smell the aroma of chocolate cookies fresh from the oven. Then there were the songs! Mother was always singing, and teaching us funny little tunes and Bible songs. In our house the children were included in adult conversations on an equal basis and we were allowed, encouraged, to handle cherished books. There were trays in bed when we were sick and sometimes just because we needed a little extra coddling. Even the negatives were handled in a positive way. Once I got a D on my report card; I don't remember the subject now, but I had been ill and missed school. The teacher said, "Just wait till you get home and your parents see that D." The teacher was trying to shame me, but I wasn't afraid to bring the report card home, and didn't expect a big scolding because we had never had anything but loving support in all we did. Dad looked at the card, mused for a moment and said, "Well, D must stand for 'Dandy!'" I'm sure I got a little extra help and tutoring in the offending subject, but there was no expressed disapproval.

Life was real. It wasn't always a bowl of cherries without pits. But the pits were faced and dealt with. Because I grew up in a basically happy home, I assumed, perhaps naively, that everyone would naturally love, care for, and cherish their parents or other family elders. It's easy to love lovable people, but some have grown up in homes where love was not expressed openly, where accomplishments were the basis for approval, where demands and expectations of perfection obscured any expressions of love. Unfortunately, many have even experienced abuse at the hands of their parents. Surely we cannot ask those people to love and cherish and protect their elders now, can we?

Yes? No? Maybe so?

Family backgrounds influence every decision. No two families experience the same history, genetics, environment, or even ethics. Positive backgrounds can lead to positive feelings, and all's well. But sometimes the love experienced in positive backgrounds can lead to negative feelings because of a sense of obligation to "the norm," which can carry its own guilt trip. Obviously, negative backgrounds can lead to negative feelings because of a sense of having no responsibility to what was considered an unfavorable family history. Perhaps surprisingly, a negative history can also lead to a determination to change the cycle and overcome the minuses of the past. If, in the words of an old song, we can learn to "accentuate the positive," and "eliminate the negative" (by dealing with it), everyone benefits from the results.

Love is a choice. Too often, we can't bring out our feelings of love, and so feel guilty that we don't "love" this elder when he or she is being difficult. But love chooses to overlook the quarrelsomeness, complaining, and volatile changes in behavior. One caregiver reported taking her mother-in-law into their home out of loyalty to her husband. Although motivated by thoughts of duty to the elder, a sense of it being the right thing to do, she confessed no love for this woman who had been a gossiping, self-centered, complaining troublemaker most of her life. Elaine felt guilty because she didn't love her mother-in-law. Things were very difficult for many months until the breakthrough came, when Elaine realized she had been choosing to do the loving things, the right things, even without the feelings.

Love chooses what is right for the other person. Love chooses to be patient. Love chooses to be kind. Love chooses to put the other person first. Love chooses not to react with anger. Love chooses to overlook minor irritations and chooses not to dwell on them. Love chooses to find ways to solve major problems. Love chooses not to keep track of the other's faults. Love chooses to protect. Love chooses to trust. Love chooses to remain hopeful. Love chooses to persevere— to hang in there. Love chooses never to give up. (Does this sound familiar? It's been said before. This is the authors' paraphrase, based on their own experience, of the Apostle Paul's writings in 1 Corinthians 13, the Holy Bible.)

And in the choosing, love eventually discovers that it does truly feel love.

Alone
I walk
the peopled city.

Obadiah Milton Conover

⸘⸘

They are
never alone
that are accompanied
with noble thoughts.

Arcadia
Sir Philip Sidney
1554-1586

Seventeen

You'll Never Walk Alone

⊰ In the early days of my advocacy, I did so much by instinct alone that I often felt entirely alone. I wondered if anything I could do as a single individual would have any impact at all in the vast wilderness of elder advocacy. As I began to meet other people— and it seemed that everywhere I told my story, others would relate similar situations. I realized that I was not alone. But few of us knew what others were doing; it was by trial and error and happenstance that we discovered common bonds, common purposes, and ways of supporting one another just by the mere fact of being and doing.

Are you asking similar questions? What can one person do? What difference can it make? Why bother?

Perhaps some of the following stories will encourage you as they have me.

Life Is Not Just a Box of Chocolates

Her name was Frances Jones. I never saw her face. I never met her. She was a voice, a warm, soothing, caring voice. She'd heard me on a radio program and called to ask my advice about a minor problem she'd encountered concerning her sister, who was in a local long-term care facility. Frances was apologetic. Hers wasn't a case of physical abuse or gross neglect. It was all about a box of chocolates sent for Valentine's Day by another sister in a distant state. Only it didn't get delivered. Was there anything she could do?

I didn't consider her dilemma a minor one at all. My protective "hackles" immediately stood at alert. My mom had loved candy too.

We'd solve this mystery together! The telephone calls flew back and forth between the sisters and me.

The nursing home said no candy had ever arrived. (Case closed? Not so fast.) Sister had sent the candy by UPS. UPS had records. Frances obtained a copy of the signed delivery receipt, acknowledged by the nursing home. (Er, ah...) "But we can't read the signature. Anyone could have signed for it." (Maybe it'll go away.) I beg your pardon. (Persistence.) The nursing home, by virtue of the signed receipt, acknowledged receiving the package. Bottom line: Frances was eventually given a check for the amount of the candy plus the shipping costs. She bought a new box and brought it to her sister for a belated Valentine's Day celebration. (Victory!)

I called Frances from my office occasionally, just to see how things were going. She confided that she was receiving medical treatments, and couldn't visit her sister as often as she would like. I think our chats encouraged both of us. One day during the Christmas season, I returned to the office to find a message from Frances on my answering machine, wishing me a merry Christmas. It touched me because I knew it was a long-distance call and she had a limited income. I called to tell her how much I appreciated hearing from her. From then on she made it a point to call around any holiday. I'd pick up the phone and there she was.

"Honey, it's Frances," in that voice as warm as honey. Always concerned for my welfare, always sensitive to my moods. "Are you doing all right?" "Are you getting enough rest?"

After returning from a trip, I called to check on her but got no answer. I tried several days at different times of day, but still no answer. I was a bit apprehensive, knowing she'd been getting medical attention for an unnamed condition. Finally, with relief, I heard the telephone receiver being picked up, but an unfamiliar voice greeted me. It was Frances's daughter. Frances had passed away a few days before.

There's a Frances-sized hole in my heart, and I still miss her. She was a warm, generous lady who probably didn't think of herself as a crusader against elder abuse, but she made a difference in my life. I like to think that the encouragement she gave me helped me face many of the frustrating days I went through while trying to help other families. So her gift was multiplied many times over.

One person can make a difference!

"I Know You Can Help Me"

By the time his father passed away nine years earlier, Rick Campbell had seen enough of nursing homes to swear he'd never set foot in one again. He was relieved to be closing that chapter and looking forward to a newer, fresher phase of his life.

He was a bit disconcerted when a woman approached him in church one Sunday. "I know you can help me," she implored. "I need your help with my mother. She's in a nursing home. She speaks no English, but she's got to have some help."

"I don't know what I could do," Rick answered hesitantly.

"She wants to receive communion. I know you could help her."

"I'm not a priest," Rick answered. "I'm not qualified to give communion."

Rick couldn't get the woman off his mind. Drawn almost magnetically, he visited his priest and asked about the possibility of a layperson being trained and qualified to give communion. From that encounter, Rick became qualified to give communion, and a new ministry was born. Even though the language barrier created difficulties, the more common language of the elements of communion allowed a greater communication.

"Other people saw me serving communion and wanted to take part too," Rick explains.

"The sense of aloneness of some of these people in long-term care is overwhelming. Some have no family. Some feel abandoned. Some have outlived their friends and relatives. And some are comparatively young—victims of debilitating diseases or of accidents that have left them unable to live at home. My heart just breaks for them."

Rick's compassion has led to regular visits to as many as fifty people in several long-term care facilities. His empathetic willingness to listen has made him aware of the many little ways people can ease the pain and loneliness of the clinical warehousing we call long-term care.

"It takes so little," he continues. "One person needed a new lap robe, another wanted something to drink. Sometimes it's just the attention of a friendly face." The trunk of his car has become a treasure trove of treats and diversions he shares with his "clients."

In the course of Rick's visits, he has noticed that the young residents are housed and treated with the same regimen as the elderly, which is particularly discouraging for people whose adult lives were just beginning when they were sidelined by accident or disease over which they had no control.

"Why can't we have these young people housed together in separate facilities or at least separate wings, providing the amenities for as normal a life as possible? They'd like to have access to music and entertainment, clothing, menus, and even daily schedules to suit their tastes." Rick's dream is to see such facilities made available to younger people.

Rick's "caseload" involves daily trips to nursing homes, before and after his own regular job, and on weekends, as well. He also carries the responsibilities of a busy and diversified, but very supportive, family.

Rick didn't leave heartbreak behind after his father's death. He's had to say good-bye to a number of new friends who've passed away since he became involved in their lives. He still experiences the frustrations of trying to make things better within a sometimes-difficult system. But he's also experienced the joys of accomplishment. He was invited to tell his story to California State Senator John Lewis' task force for the elderly, and on local cable television. He was nominated for the Children's Hospital of Orange County "Heroes of the Heart Award."

"That was the greatest night of my life," he says of the awards presentation. "I'll probably never give up advocating for these people. Just when I think the load is lightening, I find new hands to hold. And I can't say no. Whether or not I can change the big picture, it takes so

little to make a difference in their lives. Anyone can do that."
One person can make a difference!

A Voice Out of the Night

Who listens to the radio in the middle of the night? In an unusual tangle of coincidence that I didn't straighten out for a while, I learned that people do, and they even call the stations! Janice Karich couldn't sleep one night and tuned in to a talk radio show for company. The topic was issues concerning the elderly. Various callers were discussing how to find a good nursing home. Janice had had a bad experience with a nursing home when her grandmother, Nana, was alive, so her ears perked up when a caller mentioned my advocacy educating people about various forms of elder abuse. Good for her, thought Janice, taking down my number.

Early the next morning, my phone rang and a friendship was born. "I heard about you on the radio last night," she began. How? I wondered. I wasn't aware of a broadcast of anything relating to NOBLE.

Although her Nana was now gone, Janice's experiences with the facility where she had been made her immediately sympathetic and supportive of NOBLE's advocacy work. After I sent her some of our informational materials, we talked often on the phone. She offered to do anything she could do from her home to help us—research, mailings, phoning. She became a one-woman clipping service, filling our files with newspaper and magazine items and articles about elder abuse. She called the radio show to inform them of our work. She wrote to Barbara Bush on my behalf, and was thrilled to receive a letter and a phone call from Randa Mendenhall, at the White House, in response. After my visit with Mrs. Bush, Randa and I called Janice to tell her about the visit.

"I'm so thrilled," Janice exclaimed. "I feel as if I'd gotten to go with you."

Janice began calling just to check on me because she sensed the pressure I was under as the NOBLE caseload increased, with calls and letters coming from all over the United States. By sharing my concern and pain over the atrocities I was hearing about, Janice was able to help me stay on an even keel. I could release my frustrations long-distance, when I chose not to do so with close family and friends. One evening as we hung up, I instinctively said, "Good night, Doll." That was a pet name my brother used to call me. There was a moment's silence on the other end. "That was what my husband used to call me," she said in a choked voice.

Janice's faith has kept her strong through many trials—through the death of her Nana, the death of her husband, and now, finally, in her own severe illness. She is still giving, still concerned about my interests, my work, and my well-being.

I met her only once. Shortly after our first contact, she attended one of my early NOBLE meetings. I opened the meeting disappointed, thinking she wasn't going to be able to make it after all. When the small attractive woman walked in late, I knew from her smile that it had to be Janice. She brought a warm glow into the room and I knew then that we were truly friends.

She was a constant gift to me, and the gift continues even now, after her death. One person can make a difference!

"Anything...anything..."

The attitude that most characterizes Pat Valdez is "There's a right way and a wrong way to do things. If it's wrong, it's got to be fixed." When Pat first stepped through the doors of my office at NOBLE, I read in her eyes a steely determination that only hinted at the trauma she had experienced. Like many of us involved in this work, Pat experienced elder abuse firsthand while overseeing her aunt's care. In an eighteen-month period, her aunt resided in six long-term care facilities where she experienced abuse, neglect, and over-medication, till she had to be sent to a psychiatric facility for detoxification. She then had extreme difficulty finding a bed in a facility that would allow her to transfer from a psychiatric facility. The locked facility looked substandard, and it was with misgivings that Pat allowed her aunt to be placed there. Her intuition proved reliable: within two weeks her aunt was beaten. Once again there was a desperate search for another facility. According to the administrator of one long-term care facility to which she applied, it is not uncommon for there to be "no available beds" for residents coming out of psychiatric facilities, regardless of the fact that their condition was caused by over-medication prescribed in another facility. Another locked substandard facility was found. A bowel problem, neglected by that facility for eighteen days, led to a blockage for which she had to be hospitalized. There she developed a decubitis ulcer (bedsore) and a contagious pneumonia-like condition that antibiotics would not clear and because of which the facility refused to accept her back into their care. Another search, another facility!

Pat's aunt had died by the time we met, but the hurt and outrage were still very close to the surface. When she saw a newspaper article about NOBLE, she decided to put her frustration to work in a positive direction. She offered to do anything I needed for the office, typing at home after her own workday ended. We often met in the mutually convenient parking lot of a local furniture store; I'd hand the work to her one evening, and the next she'd hand the finished work back to me. It was "Hi," "Thanks," and "Good-bye."

When I began doing presentations for various groups and organizations, Pat agreed to tell her story and allowed us to use the pictures of her aunt's abuse. She testified before a public hearing called by California Assemblyman Gil Ferguson. She became an invaluable member of the board of directors of NOBLE, and until the doors were forced to close for lack of funding, her prevailing attitude was, "If you ever need me for anything—anything, call me. I'll do it."

One person can make a difference!

It Had to be Fate

"I believe you," said the warm voice on the other end of the line. I was so prepared to offer documented explanations that her immediate affirmation left me speechless. "I've been there. Nothing surprises me anymore." I felt her empathy immediately.

That was my introduction to Carole Herman, founder of FATE (Foundation Aiding the Elderly), in Sacramento, California. After her aunt died in a long-term care facility, following gross neglect of decubitis ulcers, Carole's fighting instinct led her to establish FATE, where she has been working to make a difference for more than sixteen years. She has been a serious advocate for the elderly, educating herself and then others about the maze of officialdom regulating care facilities throughout the state, pushing for reform, for enforcement of present laws, for necessary new laws, and encouraging novice advocates like me. Carole had "been there, done that" and was unhesitatingly generous with helpful suggestions. From my first little office in the guest bedroom of my home, I found myself calling her frequently for advice. I appreciated and respected the fact that she would advocate for anyone who needed assistance. As we became better acquainted, and realized our goals and purposes and operating styles were compatible, we ended up serving on one another's boards of directors. In attempting to carry the message of elder abuse to the widest possible audience, each of us often advocated for the other's work. A personal friendship also developed, which has extended to our husbands.

Every advocate needs, but does not always have, personal contact with another advocate. The mutual encouragement, strength, and support are benefits no one else can provide with the same degree of empathy. Carole is a wife, mother, grandmother, and the vice-president of her own software company—extraordinary in what she does, but ordinary in that she is one individual doing what she can, to the best of her ability. In her, as in so many others who have experienced the outrage of elder abuse, runs that common thread of needing to do something, and to pass along any assistance that is in her power to give.

"Closure (of your own case) is really only the beginning of advocacy for others," she says.

One person can make a difference!

THE JOURNEY IS NOT COMPLETE

Elder abuse respects no one. It didn't matter that Sandra Hagan was a strong, articulate, bank vice-president who had placed her mother in what she believed was "the finest skilled care facility in the area." Her mother's neglect and subsequent death from sepsis (major infection) caused by dry gangrene hit Sandra hard, to say the least.

An ombudsman had given her my name. As with so many people who came to my office, there was that expression in her eyes. She knew she needed to do something to have closure. The local Department of Health Services—Licensing and Certification office had issued a Class B citation with a thousand-dollar fine, but this was an unacceptably light judgment in view of her mother's death.

We discussed options. I explained that the founding of NOBLE was my route to closure, and that I wanted no other frail elderly person to suffer what my mother had endured.

"That's what I want," Sandra said, echoing so many for whom there had been no help.

At NOBLE I had established a small ritual of presenting new clients with a symbol of hope and happiness: a tiny glass bluebird, to remind them of our friendship and advocacy. At that first meeting, I wanted Sandra to fully understand the depth of my concern for her and her situation. As I handed her the sparkling little memento, she knew she had a friend.

In the ensuing months, Sandra became not only a valuable friend, but a member of my board of directors as well. Her route to closure has taken several paths. Through the auspices of her church, she teaches a course titled "Honor Your Father and Mother, for Middle Adults who Love and Care for Older Adults." (©1989 by Graded Press, Nashville, TN.) The course investigates various aspects of "the sandwich generation" dealing with elder care. She suggests to those who take the course (usually church groups, Sunday school classes, etc.) that they form a support group to "adopt" a nursing home.

As was her right, Sandra contested the original finding, and eventually a Class A citation, carrying a penalty of $10 thousand, was issued against the facility. In a conversation with one of the official offices involved in the investigation, a person who will remain unnamed said, "I thank you and my family thanks you." Because Sandra felt that the facility where her mother died had not really "gotten the message," and she had no certainty there would be real change, she brought suit against them.

"I guess," she says hopefully, "the bottom line is, I'm on a mission and the journey is not complete."

Patience and perseverance.

One person can make a difference!

The Dream Team

"What luck!" "Talk about being in the right place at the right time!" "Talk about knowing the right people!" "Talk about a dream job in a dream location!" We throw those cliches around a lot when we don't know quite how to explain the combination of circumstances that results in something wonderful.

Randa Mendenhall is the first to admit to "all of the above" when it comes to her work in the White House. But we know there was more to it: there was ability; there was efficiency and proficiency; there was preparation and patience and persistence. When, after spending several years abroad, Randa returned to the United States, she knew she'd like to work either in California or Washington, D. C. It seemed to be an arbitrary decision to choose Washington.

Randa had defined her dream job as working in one of the foreign ambassadorial offices or an international corporation, where she could use her proficiency in several languages. But she began questioning her choice of Washington when, after forty-five interviews in two and a half weeks, her dream job hadn't yet materialized. A friend suggested she take the civil service entrance exam just to see what might be available in other fields.

Returning home one day, she found a message from the White House on her answer machine. "In the crazy bustle of the past weeks, my brain didn't really register the message. I assumed it was from the White House Hamburger Corporation, so I hadn't yet returned the call." A frantic call came later from a friend who worked on the White House staff, saying that Mrs. Pat Nixon's office had a position for her. At the age of twenty-four, Randa was hired as social correspondent to the First Lady!

Seventeen years later, another "friend in high places" encouraged her to apply as a volunteer on Mrs. Barbara Bush's staff. Although she was working as director of special events for Reston Town Center Associates, a subsidiary of Mobil Land Development, Randa retained one day a week for volunteer work, and for four great years she worked in the special projects office for Mrs. Bush.

It was during that time that I met Randa Mendenhall, who responded graciously to my correspondence with Mrs. Bush about NOBLE, bringing my advocacy work to Mrs. Bush's attention, being the intermediary for our correspondence, and opening the doors for my invitation to the White House. That appointment has lent great credibility to my work, and for that I am very grateful, both to Mrs. Bush and to Randa Mendenhall. For me Randa was "the right person in the right place at the right time."

Not everyone can work in the White House. Not everyone can volunteer at the White House.

But one person can make a difference!

WE'VE BEEN WALKING ALONE...TOGETHER

I can't address this to you by name—I never knew your name. At the time I wanted to know. I wanted to confront you, to demand reasons and answers. But my reasoning side knew I was too full of rage to handle that sort of encounter. Through my anguish and anger I knew it was better not to face you.

But you changed my life. Nothing was the same after that. It was a big change knowing that my precious mother was no longer there for me, and would never be there for me again. It was a big change going through the frustrations of trying to see that nothing like this ever again happened to anyone's mother—even yours. It was a change meeting people I'd never had any reason to meet before. It was a change becoming the type of person bold enough to speak out about the unacknowledged problem of abuse of our elder generation. It was a change learning the ropes of advocacy work, facing government representatives, attempting to work with industry representatives, hearing the heartbreaking stories of far too many families who had experienced far too many incidents similar to mine.

But you did change my life. With the help of many others I have been able to help many families. In the short time NOBLE's doors were open, I heard from hundreds of families in thirty-eight states, detailing all sorts of abuse from all sorts of people like you all over the United States. And I know my experiences represent just the tip of the iceberg of a chilling national disgrace.

It has been years since you began these changes in my life, since my mother died six weeks after you beat her. And now, after all that has happened in these past twelve years, I sense a new change in my life.

And you're involved in that too. It's not complete yet. I'm not sure it ever will be. I'm told that for my own sake it must become complete. A friend told me, "It's called forgiveness." "I know," I responded, "I think it's coming. I'm working on it."

You did something for me. You triggered a strength that I didn't know I had. You started me on a quest, in anger at first, to seek protection for others. In that quest I've learned much. As I've been able to help others, the place of anger has gradually eroded and has begun to fill with fresher waters of encouragement, and with hope that what I've experienced and written about may open the eyes of all people. You see I no longer hold you solely responsible. Oh yes, you were guilty of losing control, of battering a tiny, bed-bound, eighty-six-pound, ninety-one-year-old woman who was always a lady. And you've had to live with that (and with what else?) for many years even though you got away with it at the time. I hope that some of the things I've learned and shared in this book will help not only the elderly and their families, but the medical people who treat them, the people who establish and oversee long-term care facilities, the people who enact laws of protection, and people like you, who must learn to cope with and control your own emotions.

So you see, we do have something in common. We have "walked alone...together" for years, neither knowing the other, each of us dealing with the fallout in our separate lives from that one incident that binds us together forever. I hope you can understand that you are not alone; you no longer have to walk alone. You can reach out for help; I hope you already have. I hope, through cooperative efforts throughout the nation, there will soon be a cure for this social disease called "abuse of the elderly." I've attempted to do my part. Perhaps one day we'll realize that we all depend on each other; none of us walks alone. One person can make a difference!

What Can One Person Do?

One person can become an ombudsman. The State Department of Aging—Long-term Care Ombudsman Program exists in all fifty states, providing official representatives to protect the interests of residents of long-term care facilities and to resolve problems and complaints. Under the program's authority, volunteers are trained to function in this role. This is a positive way for any individual to make a substantial, perhaps lifesaving, difference. It is an especially vital service for residents without any family or personal advocate.

The effectiveness of this program will depend upon the cooperative efforts and goals of the director, the paid staff, the volunteers, and
the volunteer board of directors. As a board member of the Orange
County Council on Aging (CA), I had the privilege of serving with
Pamala McGovern, a leader of principle and integrity, dedicated solely
to the interests of the residents in long-term care facilities. While the
tone set by the director is important, the positive influence and efforts of a volunteer can make a significant difference, even in negative
situations. If just one resident is helped, it is more than worth it.

One person can make a difference!

One Person Can:

"Adopt" a resident in a long-term care facility. Discover a resident
who has few or no visitors. Visit. Send cards. Bring a flower. Sit and
hold a hand, even if there is little response.

Become a "student." Learn all you can about elder issues in your area.
Start a clipping file for an advocacy group or a legislator. Be sure to clip
the news source (newspaper or magazine name and date) for each item.

Volunteer at a local senior citizen's center, day care center, or long-
term care facility.

Write letters: To the newspaper editor, to elected officials, to long-
term care facility residents, or for residents unable to write their own
letters. Seek out residents whose family might live at a distance, in
another town or state. Write for the resident, to keep the family aware
of the resident's activities, general condition, and care. This point of
contact could be a real service to a concerned daughter or son in another
state. And wouldn't it be great if you could encourage the family in
another state to visit an elder in one of their local facilities, to do the
same thing for someone else's parent! Personal initiative in networking could improve conditions for a lot of people.

Help the activities director at a long-term care facility: Teach a craft.
Play the piano for their sing-along.

Join a clowning club that visits long-term care facilities.

Join Hugs for Health, a volunteer organization in California that teaches and shares the art of hugging, offering much-needed nurture for residents of senior care facilities. (Jo Lindberg, founder/president, Box 1704, Tustin, CA 92681; (714) 832-4847; Fax: (714) 516-9078; www.hugs4health.org.)

Enlist your teenagers. Enlist their social and service groups. Their vivacity and enthusiasm are contagious.

Invite knowledgeable speakers to address your class, your church, your club, your business, on subjects of concern to elders and the sandwich generation.

Be a support to advocates. Write or telephone. Encourage. Listen.

One person—a member of a class, a church group, a philanthropic organization or service club—can encourage the group to become informed, to take a stand, to initiate new projects of involvement and support, to contribute financially to an advocacy organization, or take part in any of the activities listed above. We call these PEP Groups (People Encouraging Participation). See Appendix J for suggestions.

One person in a professional capacity—physician, attorney, legislator, legislative assistant, clergy person, businessman or woman—can go the extra mile in advocacy for the elderly. Consider how you may be able to support an advocate or an advocacy group through your training, your support, your expertise, your advice, perhaps your participation on a board of directors. I have experienced supportive help from people in each of these categories.

What can one person do?

There is an often-quoted prayer by theologian Reinhold Niebuhr: "O God, give us serenity to accept what cannot be changed, courage to change what should be changed, and wisdom to distinguish the one from the other."

To which we add, "But God, grant us the courage not to give up on what we think is right, even though we may think it is hopeless."

One person *can* make a difference!

Plus one, and one, and one.

And you'll never walk alone.

Appendices

Appendix A

Notes

Long-term Care Resident: The term "resident" rather than "patient" is used throughout the field of elder care, regarded as affording more dignity to the elder. The term is used in like manner throughout this book, except in discussing the doctor/patient relationship.

Nursing Home: Rather than choosing a fictitious name that might coincide with an existing facility, we have used the generic term "nursing home" for the long-term care facility where Sandell's mother was beaten. This is not necessarily to protect the facility, as the events that transpired there are a matter of the investigative records of several agencies. Because the problem of elder abuse is so widespread throughout the nation, the generic name suggests the need for consumers to make every effort to determine the quality of any facility under consideration, regardless of its reputation.

New Facility: The generic title, "new facility," where Sandell's mother was moved after the abuse, was chosen for similar reasons. There are progressive facilities that provide excellent care and make every effort to protect residents in all aspects of care. The generic term "new facility" is intended to represent those kinds of facilities.

Ombudsman: Long-term Care Ombudsman Services are available in every state, found in the telephone book under government (county or state) listings, "Area Agency on Aging." An ombudsman is an impartial mediator, an advocate, mandated by state and federal law, of basic human rights of long-term care residents.

The California Ombudsman services

• Provide information to residents and their families to assist in their selection of a long-term care facility—not offered by all California Ombudsman programs.
• Build a trusting relationship with the resident and help foster peace of mind.
• Investigate and help resolve complaints of neglect and abuse—mandated.
• Assist residents with resources for help with personal finances and legal problems.
• Monitor the quality of food and general health care—mandated.

Posey: A posey is a vest-like garment used to restrain the wearer in bed or in a chair. There are vastly differing opinions about their use. Those who favor it cite the protection factor to prevent falls. Those opposed suggest that the restraint may itself cause undue agitation, and entanglement leading to potential injury and even death. Certainly it restricts movement, leading to atrophy of bones and muscles, constipation, etc.

Case Histories: Except where permission has been granted to cite specific cases, details of cases have been modified to represent typical examples of abuse, common to an appalling number of situations nationwide.

Fictitious Names: Throughout the narrative, the names of some physicians, nurses, and long-term care residents have been changed to protect the privacy of those individuals.

Appendix B

What Is Abuse?

Abuse: 1. A corrupt practice or custom. 2. Improper use or treatment: misuse. 3. A deceitful act: deception. 4. Abusive language. 5. Physical maltreatment. (Webster's Seventh New Collegiate Dictionary, 1963)

Categories of Elder Abuse:

Physical Abuse: Assault and battery, slapping, beating, pinching, inflicting unnecessary pain, intentional overuse or under-use of medication, improper use of restraints, rape or sexual abuse. Watch for bruises, restraint marks, attitude changes, withdrawal, listlessness, unusual confusion, combativeness, fear, accusations, and negative reactions to facility personnel.

Mental Abuse: Threats, shouting, isolation, intimidation, ignoring. Watch for fear, withdrawal, crying, clinging, cringing, negative reactions to facility personnel, and wanting to die.

Neglect: Ignoring needs, delaying care, withholding food or water or medical treatment, withholding assistance with personal hygiene, failure to protect from harm. Watch for skin condition—tears, redness, decubitis ulcers (bedsores), dirty nails, unkempt hair, bad odors, dirty clothing, dirty or wet bed linen. Physical signs: weight loss, dehydration, listlessness, wandering.

Financial Abuse: Theft, misuse of funds, misuse of property. For the protection of assets, seek professional assistance.

Appendix C

Reference Chapter Fifteen, Paragraph A

Durable Power Of Attorney For Health Care

(California Civil Code Section 2500)

Warning to Person Executing This Document

This is an important legal document that is authorized by the Keene Health Care Agent Act. Before executing this document, you should know these important facts:

This document gives the person you designate as your agent (the attorney in fact) the power to make health care decisions for you. Your agent must act consistently with your desires as stated in this document or otherwise made known.

Except as you otherwise specify in this document, this document gives your agent the power to consent to your doctor not giving treatment or stopping treatment necessary to keep you alive.

Notwithstanding this document, you have the right to make medical and other health care decisions for yourself so long as you can give informed consent with respect to the particular decision. In addition, no treatment may be given to you over your objection at the time, and health care necessary to keep you alive may not be stopped or withheld if you object at the time.

This document gives your agent authority to consent, to refuse to consent, or to withdraw consent to any care, treatment, service, or procedure to maintain, diagnose, or treat a physical or mental condition. This power is subject to any statement of your desires and any limitations that you include in this document. You may state in this document any types of treatment that you do not desire. In addition, the court can take away the power of your agent to make health care decisions for you if your agent (1) authorizes anything that is illegal, (2) acts contrary to your known desires, or (3) where your desires are not known, does anything that is clearly contrary to your best interests.

You have the right to revoke the authority of your agent by notifying your agent or your treating doctor, hospital, or other health care provider orally or in writing of the revocation.

Your agent has the right to examine your medical records and to consent to their disclosure unless you limit this right in this document.

Unless you otherwise specify in this document, this document gives your agent the power after you die to (1) authorize an autopsy, (2) donate your body or parts thereof for transplant or therapeutic or educational or scientific purposes, and (3) direct the disposition of your remains.

This document revokes any prior durable power of attorney for health care.

You should carefully read and follow the witnessing procedure described at the end of this form. This document will not be valid unless you comply with the witnessing procedure.

If there is anything in this document that you do not understand, you should ask a lawyer to explain it to you.

Your agent may need this document immediately in case of an emergency that requires a decision concerning your health care. Either keep this document where it is immediately available to your agent and alternate agents or give each of them an executed copy of this document. You may also want to give your doctor an executed copy of this document.

Durable Power Of Attorney For Health Care

Sample

(This is provided as a sample only, and is not intended to be copied directly. It is recommended that you contact your own attorney to prepare a document to meet your specific needs and wishes.)

Article i.

Appointment Of Attorney-in-fact

I,_____ (hereinafter sometimes referred to as "Principal"), appoint as my Attorney-in-Fact_____(hereinafter referred to as "Attorney"). If the person appointed as Attorney should at any time for any reason be unable or unwilling to act or to continue to act as Attorney, then I appoint as Attorney the person(s) named as "Successor Attorney-in-Fact."

Effective Date

This Durable Power of Attorney shall become effective upon the incapacity of the Principal.

Severability

In the event that any provision herein is invalid, the remaining provisions shall nonetheless be in full force and effect.

Article ii.

Durable Power Of Attorney For Health Care

I wish to live and enjoy life as long as possible but I do not wish to receive futile medical treatment, which I define as treatment that will provide no benefit to me and will only postpone my inevitable death or prolong my irreversible coma. I desire that my wishes be carried out through the authority given to my Attorney-in-Fact (as designated herein) by this document despite any contrary feelings, beliefs or opinions of other members of my family, of relatives or of friends.

Power To Exercise Health Care Decisions

My Attorney may make health care decisions for me to the same extent as I would make health care decisions for myself if I had the capacity to do so, including but not limited to consenting to health care, or consenting to the withholding or withdrawal of health care necessary to keep me alive.

Duration

This Durable Power of Attorney for Health Care shall expire at such time as may be determined by the law, unless at such expiration date I lack the capacity to make health care decisions for myself, in which case this Durable Power of Attorney for Health Care shall continue in effect until the time when I regain the capacity to make health care decisions for myself.

Medical Records

My Attorney shall have the same right as I have to receive information regarding the proposed health care, to receive and review medical records, and to consent to the disclosure of medical records.

Refusal Or Maximization Of Medical Treatment

In exercising the authority given to my Attorney herein, my Attorney should try to discuss with me the specifics of any proposed decision regarding my medical care and treatment if I am able to communicate in any manner, even by blinking my eyes. My Attorney is further instructed that if I am unable to give an informed consent to medical treatment, my desires as stated in my "**Declaration to Withhold Life-sustaining Treatment**" shall prevail over any other provision, expressed or implied in this Durable Power of Attorney for Health Care, and my Attorney shall give or withhold such consent for me based upon the said **Declaration**. If my Attorney cannot determine the treatment choice I would want made upon the circumstances, then my Attorney should make such choice for me based upon what my Attorney believes to be in my best interests. Accordingly, if:

1. Two (2) licensed physicians who are familiar with my condition have diagnosed and noted in my medical records that my condition is incurable, terminal and expected to result in my death within twelve (12) months regardless of what medical treatment I may receive, and they have determined that I am unable to give informed consent to medical treatment; or

2. Two (2) licensed physicians who are familiar with my condition have diagnosed and noted in my medical records that I have been in a coma for at least fifteen (15) days and that the coma is irreversible, meaning that there is no reasonable possibility of my ever regaining consciousness, then my Attorney is authorized as follows:

(1) To sign on my behalf any documents necessary to carry out the authorizations described below, including waivers or releases of liability required by any health care provider,

(2) To give or withhold consent to any medical care or treatment, to revoke or change any consent previously given or implied by law for any medical care or treatment, and to arrange for my placement in or removal from any hospital, convalescent home, hospice or other medical facility, and

(3) To require that medical treatment which will only prolong my inevitable death or irreversible coma (including by way of example only such treatment as cardiopulmonary resuscitation, surgery, dialysis, the use of a respirator, blood transfusions, antibiotics, antiarrhythmic and pressor drugs or transplants) not be instituted or, if previously instituted, to require that it be discontinued.

(4) To require that procedures used to provide me with nourishment and hydration (including, for example, parenteral feeding, intravenous feedings, misting, and endotracheal or nasogastric tube use) not be instituted or, if previously instituted, to require that they be discontinued, but only if the two (2) physicians described above

also determine that I will not experience excessive pain as a result of the withdrawal of nourishment or hydration.

ARTICLE III.

Revocation Of Prior Powers Of Attorney
This power of Attorney revokes any prior Durable Power of Attorney for Health Care, executed previously by Principal.

ARTICLE IV.

Signature By Attorney
When signing on behalf of Principal under this Power of Attorney, Attorney shall sign as follows: "_____ by _____, his/her Attorney-in-Fact."

Appendix D

Reference Chapter Fifteen, Paragraph D

Evaluating And Choosing
A Long-term Care Facility

Before Placing a Loved One:

Before choosing a long-term care facility, visit as many facilities as possible. Obtain recommendations from anyone you know who has experience with local facilities—friends, acquaintances, medical personnel, clergy. The ombudsman office is a good source of information because they visit all the facilities on a regular basis; however, they do not make specific recommendations of facilities. (See Appendix A for a detailed description of the ombudsman function.)

Keep a record of your answers to the following questions, and then compare the lists.

A. Location
Location should not be the sole factor in choosing a facility; however, successful monitoring of your loved one's care will depend, to some degree, upon your ability to visit frequently, to get there quickly in case of need, to drop in unannounced and at varying times of day.

B. First Contact
  1. Why did you choose to visit this facility?
     Recommended by:
     Distance from home:
     Cost factor:
  2. Did you schedule your visit by phone?

First contact positive:

Personnel friendly, well informed:

3. First impressions of facility

Clean? Does it have an odor? In caring for incontinent residents there are bound to be times when an odor is inevitable but it should be isolated in location and duration. An overpowering scent of deodorizer is not good.

Are grounds and rooms well cared for?

Pleasant atmosphere?

4. Facility Tour

Ask to see whole facility. There should be no off-limits, except for resident privacy.

Ask to see the ombudsman poster: the poster, with telephone number, should be prominently displayed, in full view of public and residents.

Ask about latest licensing inspection report. By law it must be made available to you.

Does there seem to be adequate staff? Is the staff pleasant? How does the staff greet you? How do they treat residents? Notice the nursing stations: Lots of call buttons ringing? Staff responding?

Insufficient staff on hand? Staff loitering around station?

Residents

Are residents well groomed? Notice hands and fingernails.

Are call buttons within reach? Are they plugged in?

Are water pitchers within reach? Filled with fresh water?

Are residents responsive? Contented? Lots of sleepers?

5. Food Service (If your first visit doesn't coincide with mealtime, plan a second.)

Is dining room pleasant? Are meals attractive?

Do residents seem to be enjoying meals?

Ask to see trays for room-bound residents. Are they attractive?

Are room-bound residents eating? Are trays simply left on

bedside tables? Is there any assistance provided for those who
need it? Are sluggish eaters encouraged to eat? Any additional
snacks available at other than meal times?

6. Activities

Is there an activities director?

Schedule of activities posted?

Residents participating?

7. Services

Barber and beautician services available by appointment?

Podiatrist available by appointment?

Personal laundry service?

Plan to drop by, unscheduled, to observe consistency of above.

8. Make follow-up visit(s) using same guidelines.

Appendix E

Personal Consumer Rights Of The Elder Resident

Personal consumer rights of elder residents of long-term care facilities in California are listed in Barclays California Code of Regulations (Title 22, Section 72527), and enumerated below. The Ombudsman program in your state can inform you of regulations applying in your state.

(a) Patients have the rights enumerated in this section and the facility shall ensure that these rights are not violated. The facility shall establish and implement written policies and procedures which include these rights and shall make a copy of these policies available to the patient and to any representative of the patient. The policies shall be accessible to the public upon request. Patients shall have the right:

1. To be fully informed, as evidenced by the patient's written acknowledgement prior to or at the time of admission and during the stay, of these rights and of all rules and regulations governing patient conduct.

2. To be fully informed, prior to or at the time of admission and during the stay, of services available in the facility, and of related charges, including any charges for services not covered by the facility's basic per diem rate or not covered under Titles XVIII or XIX of the Social Security Act.

3. To be fully informed by a physician of his or her total health status and to be afforded the opportunity to participate on an immediate and ongoing basis in the total plan of care including the identification of medical, nursing and psychosocial needs and the planning of related services.

4. To consent to or to refuse any treatment or procedure or participation in experimental research.

5. To receive all information that is material to an individual patient's

decision concerning whether to accept or refuse any proposed treatment or procedure. The disclosure of material information for administration of psychotherapeutic drugs or physical restraints or the prolonged use of a device that may lead to the inability to regain use of normal bodily function shall include the disclosure of information listed in Section 72528(b).

6. To be transferred or discharged only for medical reasons, or the patient's welfare or that of other patients or for nonpayment for his or her stay and to be given reasonable advance notice to ensure orderly transfer or discharge. Such actions shall be documented in the patient's health record.

7. To be encouraged and assisted throughout the period of stay to exercise rights as a patient and as a citizen, and to this end to voice grievances and recommend changes in policies and services to facility staff and/or outside representatives of the patient's choice, free from restraint, interference, coercion, discrimination, or reprisal.

8. To manage personal financial affairs, or to be given at least a quarterly accounting of financial transactions made on the patient's behalf should the facility accept written delegation of this responsibility subject to the provisions of Section 72529.

9. To be free from mental and physical abuse.

10. To be assured confidential treatment of financial and health records and to approve or refuse their release, except as authorized by law.

11. To be treated with consideration, respect and full recognition of dignity and individuality, including privacy in treatment and in care of personal needs.

12. Not to be required to perform services for the facility that are not included for therapeutic purposes in the patient's plan of care.

13. To associate and communicate privately with persons of the patient's choice, and to send and receive personal mail unopened.

14. To meet with others and participate in the activities of social, religious and community groups.

15. To retain and use personal clothing and possessions as space

permits, unless to do so would infringe upon the health, safety or rights of the patient or other patients.

16. If married, to be assured privacy for visits by the patient's spouse and if both are patients in the facility, to be permitted to share a room.

17. To have daily visiting hours established.

18. To have visits from members of the clergy at any time at the request of the patient or the patient's representative.

19. To have visits from persons of the patient's choosing at any time if the patient is critically ill, unless medically contraindicated.

20. To be allowed privacy for visits with family, friends, clergy, social workers or for professional or business purposes.

21. To have reasonable access to telephones and to make and receive confidential calls.

22. To be free from any requirement to purchase drugs or rent or purchase medical supplies or equipment from any particular source in accordance with the provisions of Section 1320 of the Health and Safety Code.

23. To be free from psychotherapeutic drugs and physical restraints used for the purpose of patient discipline or staff convenience and to be free from psychotherapeutic drugs used as a chemical restraint as defined in Section 72018, except in an emergency which threatens to bring immediate injury to the patient or others. If a chemical restraint is administered during an emergency, such medication shall be only that which is required to treat the emergency condition and shall be provided in ways that are least restrictive of the personal liberty of the patient and used only for a specified and limited period of time.

24. Other rights as specified in Health and Safety Code, Section 1599.1.

25. Other rights as specified in Welfare and Institutions Code, Sections 5325 and 5325.1, for persons admitted for psychiatric evaluations or treatment.

26. Other rights as specified in Welfare and Institutions Code Sections 4502, 4503 and 4505 for patients who are developmentally disabled as defined in Section 4512 of the Welfare and Institutions Code.

(b) A patient's rights, as set forth above, may only be denied or limited if such denial or limitation is otherwise authorized by law. Reasons for denial or limitation of such rights shall be documented in the patient's health record.

(c) If a patient lacks the ability to understand these rights and the nature and consequences of proposed treatment, the patient's representative shall have the rights specified in this section to the extent the right may devolve to another, unless the representative's authority is otherwise limited. The patient's incapacity shall be determined by a court in accordance with state law or by the patient's physician unless the physician's determination is disputed by the patient or patient's representative.

(d) Persons who may act as the patient's representative include a conservator, as authorized by Parts 3 and 4 of Division 4 of the Probate Code (commencing with Section 1800), a person designated as attorney in fact in the patient's valid durable power of attorney for health care, patient's next of kin, other appropriate surrogate decisionmaker designated consistent with statutory and case law, a person appointed by a court authorizing treatment pursuant to Part 7 (commencing with Section 3200) of Division 4 of the Probate Code, or, if the patient is a minor, a person lawfully authorized to represent the minor.

(e) Patient's rights policies and procedures established under this section concerning consent, informed consent and refusal of treatments or procedures shall include, but not be limited to the following:

(1) How the facility will verify that informed consent was obtained or a treatment or procedure was refused pertaining to the administration of psychotherapeutic drugs or physical restraints or the prolonged use of a devise that may lead to the inability of the patient to regain the use of a normal bodily function.

(2) How the facility, in consultation with the patient's physician, will identify consistent with current statutory case law, who may serve as a patient's representative when an incapacitated patient has no conservator or attorney in fact under a valid Durable Power of Attorney for Health Care.

While these are the basic rights of residents in long-term care facilities as cited in California law, there is other information pertaining to rights and treatment of residents in other sections of this Title 22 document. If you have questions concerning rights in other states, we suggest you contact your local ombudsman for clarification of specific points.

Appendix F

Reference Chapter Fifteen, Paragraph E

Five-star Plan Assessment Meeting

Sample Meeting Agenda

The initial meeting required by OBRA (Omnibus Budget Reconciliation Act of 1987, a federal regulation containing major nursing home reforms, primarily in the area of residents' rights), may not follow this specific agenda. The Five-Point Plan, including the meeting agenda, was designed by the authors for the nonprofit corporation, NOBLE—Network Outreach Better Living for the Elderly—to address problem solving either before or after placement. Our recommendations may be adapted to meet your specific needs.

RE: Mrs. Suzy Jones   DATE:

PLACE: Request Appropriate Office   TIME:

CALLED BY: Annie Jones, Caregiver (daughter-in-law)

Introduction Of Representatives To Be Present
(List from Chapter Fifteen, Paragraph E)
1. Family Member Caregiver
2. Advocate for Resident, Ombudsman
3. Advocate for Family
4. Administrator of Facility
5. Medical Professional

Concerns To Be Discussed
(Examples: List any questions, special requirements, concerns; i.e., any family history that might have a bearing on resident's condition, fears and idiosyncrasies, personal habits or desires, medical questions

189

re treatments, things caregiver has learned at home that might benefit facility or prevent misunderstandings, etc.)

(If the meeting is to resolve a specific problem after admission, list problem(s), any actions previously discussed with, or requested of, appropriate facility personnel, verified by journal entries—see Chapter Eleven, "Attention, Please, Families, "Partnering With Long Term Care Facilities."

Example: "Before placing Mother here, I requested this, yet three times I have found her being bathed by a male CNA. I discussed this with the director of nursing on 4/23 and 5/2 [journal entry].)

SPECIFIC ACTIONS OR REQUESTS AS RESULT OF DISCUSSION
(Examples: Excessive distracting noise—radio, television, traffic— makes resident nervous and agitated. Request bed away from door, or room away from hub of activity, etc.)

(Mrs. Jones very private person, dignity important. Request all staff to address as Mrs. Jones, refrain from first name usage.)

(Mrs. Jones extremely modest. Please use only female aides in personal care—bathing, toilet assistance, etc.)

(Mrs. Jones has indicated desire and signed authorization for "no heroic action" in the event of medical emergency, etc.)

(List date of request, action agreed to, save agenda for follow up and records.)

CLOSING
(Thank all present for their time and attention.)

(Emphasize the importance of being notified regarding any details of care, willingness to come at any time, etc.)

Note: While these are only sample suggestions, they will trigger things that are of importance to your specific situation. The vital thing is to express your desires/requirements and to work with the facility personnel to best carry them out.

Appendix G

Sample Meeting Agenda

For Appealing Unacceptable Decision by Licensing
Follow instructions given on your disposition notification regarding scheduling such a meeting.

RE: Appeal disposition Mrs. Suzy Jones' case

DATE:

PLACE: Licensing and Certification Office (local, district, or state, depending on level of appeal)

Representatives Present

Licensing Agency Personnel

Family Member, Responsible Party

Advocate for Family (As in the Five-Point Plan Meeting, take along an objective friend who can support your position and remind you of points to present.)

Ombudsman Representative (Request the presence of this advocate.)

Agenda

Be prepared to clearly state your reason for disagreeing with the findings of the investigation. Take your photos, your care journal, any new information, and any corroborating facts.

Prepare a specific statement of what you want to see as a result of the appeal.

Ask that the case be reopened to further investigate the findings.

Closing

Thank the representatives for attending.

Ask when you might expect the findings of the new investigation.

Enter that estimate in your journal, along with any notes, questions, remarks, etc.

Appendix H

Reference Chapters Eleven and Fourteen

Establishing A Task Force On Elder Issues

Personnel
Sponsor: Any government official, legislator, mayor, governor, etc. (Example, California State Senator John Lewis)
Sponsor's Staff Person: Deputy, assistant, aide, etc.
Person to Chair: Advocate, knowledgeable in elder issues. Could be a family member advocating for abused elder. (Diane Sandell chaired Senator Lewis's Task Force for the Elderly.)
Ombudsman: Representative from local area Council on Aging Ombudsman Program,
Other members: (as available) Professional personnel (medicine, law, legislative), disease related organizations (Alzheimer's, Parkinson's, cancer, etc.), long-term care industry representative(s), civic personnel, service and philanthropic club members, media representatives, clergy, academia, active senior citizens, family members of elders
Note: The sponsor and the chairperson should collectively invite, under the sponsor's auspices and signature, representatives from the fields listed above.

Schedule
Determine workable schedule. Senator Lewis' Task Force for the Elderly met once a month for ten months; off July and August.

Agenda
We scheduled five meetings with guest speakers, alternating with five with discussion on proposed or pending legislation, information on advocacy experience and action and recommendations.

Guest speakers open up new aspects of advocacy. Possible speakers: Ombudsman; elder law attorneys; representative from attorney general's office; representative from senior legislature; visiting nurses; family members who have experienced the trauma of dealing with abuse of a loved one; sponsor of the task force, or assistant, to address progress of legislative action; representative of long-term care industry.

Calls to the sponsor's office requesting information or assistance regarding elder issues would be logged. From this information, family or caregiver representatives could be invited to attend the next meeting of the task force, to relate their experiences, present their concerns and to seek assistance from the panel of expertise represented.

The sponsor is invited, but need not attend every meeting. His/her administrative assistant may represent him. The purpose of the committee is to keep the legislative sponsor informed with current events, details, and recommendations.

Projects
The task force could:
- Maintain a log (compiled by sponsor's office) of inquiries, complaints, requests regarding elder issues, to be incorporated into the discussion and action of task force.
- Recruit volunteer news clipping services and maintain a notebook or file of news items related to elder issues.
- Follow specific stories through to determine what conclusive action is taken.
- Write letters to the media, requesting follow-up of related stories.
- Publish, with the sponsor's approval and under his signature, a periodical newsletter of issues related to elder concerns, to be mailed to the sponsor's constituents.
- Initiate recommended new or amended legislation for sponsor's consideration.

Appendix I

Reference Chapter Fifteen, Paragraph C

Starting A Caregiver Or Family Support Group

If you cannot find an existing support group in your area, consider starting one. The following suggestions are offered as "thought-starters" to assist your planning.

A. Determine the Need
You yourself need help. You can be sure others are in the same situation. Ask in every situation in which you find yourself—neighbors, friends, churches, shops, etc. Write the local newspaper asking for responses from others who would like to be in a support group.

B. Determine a Place and/or Sponsorship
Based on the response, decide how much room will be needed. Be creative in searching out possible locations. Churches, hospitals, schools, libraries, service clubs, banks, civic centers, senior citizen's centers all might have rooms available for public use. If one of these groups would offer sponsorship as a civic service, it would lend credibility to the cause, but determine what they would expect or require in return. It is best not to meet in the home of one of the caregivers, in order that the caregiver gets a break away from the home, but if that is the only way the group can meet don't discard the idea.

C. First Meeting
1. Record names, addresses, phone numbers.
2. Allow a brief sharing time.
3. Ask for list of concerns and suggested topics for discussion. Future meetings could include guest speakers on some of these topics.

4. Determine how often to meet and at what hours.

5. Determine future agendas from the list of concerns.

6. Establish a definite start/stop time, and adhere to it.

7. Recruit administrative help from the interests of those present: Phoning, scheduling, writing notes, notifying newspapers of future meetings, etc.

8. Encourage creative suggestions; discourage "dumping."

Appendix J

Reference Chapter Seventeen

STARTING A PEP (PEOPLE ENCOURAGING PARTICIPATION) CLUB

A PEP Club can be as simple or as imaginative and creative as you want it to be.

Goal: To involve as many people as possible in making life better for the elderly.

Plan: Find a need and fill it, from the simplest to the most complex.

• It can be for any age group, from pre-school classes to senior citizen's groups.

• It can be from any source of involvement: schools, churches, service clubs, neighborhood groups, employees' clubs.

• It can involve any monetary investment, from pennies to thousands of dollars.

• It can involve any time investment, from a one-time project to on-going support.

• It can involve any activity, from entertainment or easing loneliness, to political activism, i.e., a children's group can make colorful scrapbooks; an adult group can compile and maintain information files for a task force, or write letters.

• Groups could "adopt" individual long-term care facilities, cooperate with activities directors to provide friendship, fellowship, personal concern and caring.

• Use some of the ideas from the "One Person Can" section of Chapter Seventeen.

• Have a brainstorming party to discover new ones.

"...the noble man makes noble plans, and by noble deeds he stands."
Isaiah 32:8, the Holy Bible, New International Version

APPENDIX K

Reference Chapter Five

MOM JARVIS' LADIES' AID CAKE

Fills the house with the aroma of the holidays!
(Approximately seventy-seven years old, this recipe was widely circulated through the local "Ladies' Aid Society," of which Bessie Jarvis was a member. While the recipe is not original to Bessie, it became her signature offering for any holiday festivity.)
Put the following ingredients into a saucepan. Boil together for three minutes, then cool.

> 1 cup white sugar
> 1 cup water
> 2 cups raisins
> ½ cup lard or white vegetable shortening
> ¼ teaspoon grated nutmeg
> ¼ teaspoon salt
> 1 teaspoon ground cinnamon
> 1 teaspoon ground cloves
> ½ cup chopped walnuts

When cool add:

> 2 cups flour, to which has been added
> ½ teaspoon baking powder
> 1 teaspoon baking soda dissolved in ¼ cup hot water

Pour batter into greased and floured ring cake pan (angel food or bundt). Decorate top with pecan halves and maraschino cherries. Bake at 350° for 45-50 minutes. Test with toothpick. Remove from oven. Let cool for ten minutes. Loosen around edges. Invert on plate, then back onto another plate to keep the decorated side on top. Let cool completely.

INDEX

A

AB 2615, 60. *see also* Legal issues

Abuse. *see also* Bruises
  accountability for, 105
  actions required upon detection of, 91, 100
  as cause of death, 53-54, 58
  causes of, 55
  difficulty of proving, 52
  examples of, 53-54, 67
  incorrect diagnosis of, 30, 52, 53, 54, 71, 105
  physical effects of, 15, 58
  psychological effects of, 30, 33, 38-39, 40-41
  punishment as, 53
  reported cases in California, 59
  reporting requirements, 107, 116
  "unusual occurrence" designation, 116
  verbal, 54

Abuse history, effect on placement in nursing homes, 26

Acceptance, 140, 146

Accountability. *see also* Responsibility
  of nursing homes, 105, 115

Advertising materials, 138

Advocacy. *see also* Caregiver; NOBLE; Ombudsman
  discussed, 67, 71-72, 94, 113-114, 140, 164-165, 170-171
  Family Advocate, 129-130

  government committee participation, 73-74

Aides. *see also* Certified Nursing Assistants; Nurses; Nursing homes
  fingerprinting of, 60-61, 115
  interacting with, 91
  involvement in abuse, 8-12, 105, 168-169
  positive influences of, 38, 44

Alzheimer's Association Public Policy Committee (Orange County), 74

Alzheimer's Disease, coping with, 135

Anger. *see also* Emotions
  coping with, 134-135

Arkansas Public Service Television, 66

Attitudes. *see also* Emotions
  coping with, 133-135

Awareness
  based on personal experience, 1
  coping with, 135-136

B

Bathroom, resident' issues about, 39-40, 141

Behavior problems, 39-40, 98. *see also* Personality changes

The Big Picture, 66

Bruises. *see also* Abuse; Falls
  actions required upon detection of, 91, 100
  as evidence of abuse, 39, 52, 90, 141

Buck, Pearl S., 134

Bush, Mrs. Barbara, 51, 77-83, 161, 167

C

California. *see also* United States
  fingerprinting requirements, 61
  reported cases of abuse, 59-60
Campbell, Rick, 159-161
The CANHR Advocate (newsletter),
114
Caregiver. *see also* Advocacy
  abuse inflicted by, 52
  caring for, 121-123, 125,
151-153
  exchanging elders with other
caregivers, 152
  exhaustion affecting, 14, 123,
129-130
  lifestyle changes required by, 87,
134
  relationship with elder, 138-139
  relationship with family, 87-88
  response to abuse, 8-15, 25-26,
91, 162-163, 165, 168-169
  role reversal confusion, 120-121,
139-140
  support for, 121-123, 125,
151-153
Certified Nursing Assistants
(CNAs). *see also* Aides
  fingerprinting requirements, 115
  improper training of, 55
Changes, 87, 140
Checkbooks, 121, 137
Children's Hospital of Orange
County, 160
Closure. *see also* Death; Family
  advocacy as technique for, 67,
165
  after abuse, 93-94
  personal experiences of, 51
CNAs. *see* Certified Nursing

Assistants
Council on Aging (Orange
County), 73, 170
Cremation, 45

D

Death. *see also* Closure
  caused by abuse, 53-54, 58
  discussing with elder, 139
  grieving associated with, 140
Decision making skills. *see also*
Responsibility
  of caregiver, 122, 123, 127-128
  of elders, 120, 122, 127,
135-136, 138
Decubitis ulcers, 53, 54, 163
Denial, 52, 71-72
Department of Health Services,
Licensing and Certification
  citation and fine system,
114-115, 165-166
  notification procedures, 60,
73-74, 91, 93, 105, 116
Depression, 141. *see also* Emotions
Dietary deficiency, as abuse, 53, 54
Dignity, issues about, 40, 120-121,
137-138, 140-142
Dirty dozen. *see also* Frustration;
specific subjects
  awareness, 135-136
  caring for caregiver, 151-153
  dignity, 140-142
  family involvement, 136-137
  fear, 144-145
  feelings and attitudes, 133-135
  frustration, 145-148
  guilt, 148-151
  idiosyncrasies, 142-144
  love, 153-155

responsibility, 137-139
role reversal, 139-140
Disneyland Community Service
Award, 74

E
Elder. *see also* Elder care; Parents;
Resident
  living with family, 22-25
  personality changes affecting,
  120-123, 135-136
  visualizing difficulties of, 147
Elder Abuse and Dependent Adult
Civil Protection Act, 59, 116. *see
also* SB 679
Elder care
  assessing the situation, 120-123
  caring for caregiver, 123-125
  in general, 87, 119
  nursing home decisions, 126-128
  partnering with nursing home,
  128-131
  resources for, 125-126
Emotions. *see also* Feelings; Guilt
  of caregiver, 71, 124-125, 153
  effect on of physical abuse, 15
  recording in notebook, 90

F
Falls. *see also* Bruises
  abuse diagnosed as, 30, 52, 53,
  54, 71, 105
Family. *see also* Closure; Friends;
Parents; Relatives
  assumption of responsibility by,
  61, 74, 87-88, 152
  coping with involvement of,
  136-137
  denial of abuse in, 52
  healing for, 58

partnering
  with government officials,
  92-93
  with medical professionals,
  88-89
  with nursing homes, 89-91,
  128-131
  relationship with caregiver,
  87-88, 121-123
Family Circle, 67, 78
FATE. *see* Foundation Aiding the
Elderly
Fear. *see also* Idiosyncrasies;
Paranoia
  compassionate responses to, 38,
  113
  coping with, 144-145
  following death of parent, 43
  legitimate, 67, 91, 98, 136,
  137-138, 140
Feelings. *see also* Emotions; Love
  coping with, 133-135, 140
  negative, 155
Ferguson, Assblymn. Gil, 163
Financial assistance, resources for,
126
Fingerprinting. *see also* Legal issues
  of aides and CNAs, 60-61, 115
First Presbyterian Church of
Orange, 73
Forgiveness, 168-169
Foundation Aiding the Elderly
(FATE), 73
  discussed, 164-165
Fraud, in Medicare billings, 106,
115
Friends. *see also* Family
  support from, 124-125
Frustration. *see also* Dirty dozen

coping with, 40, 72, 120, 137, 145-148
Frustration box, 146-147

G

Government officials. *see also* Legal issues
    partnering with, 92-93
    recommendations for, 111-117
Grooming. *see also* Sanitary issues
    issues about, 121, 135
Guilt. *see also* Emotions
    coping with, 148-151

H

Haas, Jane Glenn, 58
Hagan, Sandra, 165
Hankin, Marc, 59, 60, 64, 65
Herman, Carole, 164-165
HHAs. *see* Home health aides
Home health aides (HHAs),
fingerprinting requirements, 115
The Home Show, 64
"Honor Your Father and Mother," 165
Hugs, 145
Hugs for Health, 170-171
Humor, 146

I

Idiosyncrasies. *see also* Fear;
Personality changes
    coping with, 142-144
Inside San Diego, 63
Investigations. *see also* Legal issues
    in general, 58-59, 60, 93
Isolation
    of caregiver, 125
    of institutionalized elders, 52, 53,

54

J

Jarvis, David, 3
Jones, Frances, 157-159
Journal. *see also* Photographs
    for meetings, 130
    for nursing home visits, 90

K

Karich, Janice, 161-162

L

Lane, Bessie
    biography, 1-4, 71, 85
    death and memorial, 43-47
    experiences of abuse, 7-15
    post-abuse recovery, 39-41
Lane, Betty, 10, 11, 46, 77, 79
Language difficulties, abuse and, 55
Legal issues. *see also* Legislators
    AB 2615, 60
    annual inspection reports, 127
    citations and fines, 114-115, 165-167
    consumer guides for, 61
    fingerprinting, 60-61
    investigations, 58-59, 60, 93
    lawsuits, 57-58, 59, 166
    legislation, 59-61
    SB 679, 59, 64, 65, 68-69, 116
    SB 945, 115
Legislators. *see also* Legal issues
    partnering with, 92-93
    recommendations for, 111-117
Lewis, Sen. John, 73, 92-93, 112, 160
Long-term care facility. *see* Nurs-

ing homes
Los Angeles, 65, 68-69
Love. *see also* Feelings
    choosing, 134, 155
    coping with, 153-155

M
McGovern, Pamala, 170
Mail, 143
Mealtimes, 106
Medi-Cal/Medicaid patients
    fraud associated with, 106, 115
    nursing home beds for, 26
    qualifying for, 60
Media
    focus on elder abuse, 51, 52,
    58-59, 63, 113, 170
    magazine articles, 67, 78
    press conferences, 65-66
    radio appearances, 66, 77
    television appearances, 63-66, 77
Medical personnel. *see also* Nurses;
Physicians
    partnering with, 88-89
    recommendations for, 97-101,
    131
Medical records
    accuracy concerns about, 100
    gaining access to, 13, 91
Medication, suggestions about,
120, 121
Mello, Sen. Henry, 59, 68
Memorial services, 47-48, 51
Men, as caregivers, 151
Mendenhall, Randa, 77-83, 161,
166-167
Mental deterioration. *see also*
Personality changes
    following abuse, 38-39

Morticians, 44-45

N
Names, using respect with, 98
Naps, 148, 150, 151
Networking, described, 73-74
Niebuhr, Reinhold, 171
Nixon, Mrs. Pat, 167
NOBLE (Network
Outreach-Better Living for the
Elderly). *see also* Advocacy
    discussed, 72-71-75, 85, 161,
    163, 165
    Five-Star Evaluation Plan
        assessing the situation,
    120-123
        caring for caregiver, 123-125
        in general, 119
        nursing home decisions,
    126-128
        partnering with nursing
    home, 128-131
        resources, 125-126
Nurses. *see also* Aides; Physicians
    in nursing homes, 90-91
Nursing home. *see also* Resident
    annual inspection reports, 127
    difficulties finding openings in,
    31-32
    difficulties with, 25-26, 67,
    106-107
    family's responsibility for
    selecting, 74, 126-128
        making decision for, 126-128
        partnering with, 89-91, 128-131
        physicians responsibility to,
    30-31
        psychiatric facility, 162-163
        relationships with staff, 90-91

responsibility of for Resident' safety, 60

Nursing home administration
  campaign contributions by, 114
  policies of, 55, 57-58
  recommendations for, 103-109
  responsibilities of, 57-58, 105-106, 131

O

OBRA. *see* Omnibus Budget Reconciliation Act

Ombudsman. *see also* Advocacy
  contacting, 91, 93, 126, 130
  discussed, 169-171

Omnibus Budget Reconciliation Act of 1987 (OBRA), 89

The Orange County Register, 58

Overcrowding, as cause of abuse, 55

P

Paranoia. *see also* Fear
  legitimate, 25
  medical help for, 145

Parents. *see also* Elder; Family
  moving to new facility, 37-38
  saying goodbye to, 43-47
  separated in different hospitals, 19-22

Patience, 144-145

Personality changes. *see also* Behavior problems; Emotions; Idiosyncrasies; Mental deterioration; Role reversal
  assessment of, 120-123
  coping with, 135-136

Photographs
  to document abuse, 10, 11,

29-30, 40, 63, 64, 91, 92, 93
  on-going procedures for, 89-90

Physical therapy, 38

Physicians. *see also* Nurses
  incorrect diagnosis by, 30, 52, 53
  partnering with, 88-89, 99
  recommendations for, 97-101
  retained by Nursing home, 29, 30-31, 88-89, 100

Police, notifying of abuse, 13-14, 91, 105

Power of Attorney, discussed, 91, 122, 138

Press conferences, 65-66

Privacy, 148, 150

Psychological effects, following abuse, 40-41

Punishments, 53

R

Rape, 54

Relatives. *see also* Family
  abuse inflicted by, 52

Resident. *see also* Elder; Nursing home
  "adopting," 170
  compassionate care of, 38
  fear of abuse, 52
  as human beings, 97, 98, 128
  no age segregation for, 160
  policy suggestions following death of, 107

Resources, for caregiver, 124-125

Respect, maintaining with elders, 98, 141-142

Responsibility. *see also* Decision making skills
  of caregiver family, 61, 87-88, 122, 127

coping with, 137-139, 151
of legislators and officials,
116-117
of nursing home management,
57-58, 105-106
Role reversal. *see also* Personality
changes
coping with, 120-121, 139-140

S

Sanitary issues, 39-40, 53, 141. *see
also* Grooming
SB 679, 59, 64, 65, 68-69, 116. *see
also* Legal issues
SB 945, 115. *see also* Legal issues
Senior centers, as resource, 124
Seymour, Sen. John, 112
Soroptimist International of
Orange, 74
Spousal Protection Against High
Cost of Long-term Care, 60
Stuckey, Meg, 32, 38
Support, 94. *see also* Advocacy;
NOBLE
  for advocates, 171
  for caregiver, 121-123, 125,
  151-153
  resources for, 126

T

Task Force committees
  participating in, 73
  suggestions for, 61, 92, 93
Theft, as form of abuse, 54,
157-159
Treats, 38
Trust, 71-72

U

United States. *see also* California
  abuse statistics, 68
  elder abuse as national disgrace,
  1, 51, 53, 63, 66
"Unusual occurrence". *see also*
Abuse; Bruises
  identification and reporting of,
  116

V

Valdez, Pat, 162

W

Wachs, Joel, 53, 66, 68-69
Wilder, Thornton, 46
Williams, Morgan, 66
Wilson, Pete, 59
Winkler, Doris, 66
Witnesses, to abuse, 12, 52